RECLAIM YOUR LIFE
FROM HOARDING

Reclaim Your Life from Hoarding

PRACTICAL STRATEGIES

for Decluttering Your Home, Organizing
Your Space, and Freeing Yourself

Eileen Dacey, MSW, LCSW

ROCKRIDGE
PRESS

For general information on our other products and services or to obtain technical support, please contact our Customer Care Department within the United States at (866) 744-2665, or outside the United States at (510) 253-0500.

Rockridge Press publishes its books in a variety of electronic and print formats. Some content that appears in print may not be available in electronic books, and vice versa.

Interior and Cover Designer: Lisa Forde

Art Producer: Samantha Ulban

Editor: Emily Angell

Production Manager: Martin Worthington

Production Editor: Melissa Edeburn

All images used under license © Shutterstock.

Author photo courtesy of © Jayne Girodat.

ISBN: Print 978-1-64611-209-8
eBook 978-1-64611-208-1

R0

TO MY LOVING HUSBAND, TIM:
Your intelligence and compassionate
spirit inspire me to pursue my dreams and
continue my efforts to advocate for the
improved well-being of vulnerable people.

TO THE PEOPLE WITH WHOM I'VE WORKED:
My growth, understanding, and experience
would not have been possible without my past
and present clients' trust and collaborative
efforts to change the narrative of hoarding
disorder. This book is dedicated to your warm
spirits, intelligence, advice, and overall hope
that recovery is possible.

Contents

Introduction

IT IS NOT UNCOMMON FOR PEOPLE TO HAVE CHALLENGES that they keep secret from others to protect themselves from judgment and scrutiny. One common secret people keep is that they have a problem with the amount of clutter they've accumulated. In fact, I've met many such people, and I have helped them find relief. In the beginning, many of the people I've worked with made great attempts to keep their problem with hoarding private. Perhaps you've been trying to mask this secret, which might be one reason you bought this book. I'm glad you're here to gain some insight into why you hoard and to learn strategies to reduce the clutter, enlist help if needed, organize your possessions, and get your home (and your life) back. Before we embark on this journey, however, I want to demystify hoarding.

When you hear the word *hoarding,* do you think of those popular reality shows with eccentric people fluttering through mounds of trash in overpacked houses while finding excuses to hold on to irreparable objects that appear to have little intrinsic value? These individuals represent only one end of the spectrum of people with hoarding problems.

For millennia, both humans and animals have hoarded food and objects for various reasons, including scarcity and deprivation. Simply stated, hoarding is the act of collecting and accumulating things. An excess of accumulated items becomes clutter. In this book, I'll refer to hoarding and cluttering interchangeably, but with the understanding that there are differences between hoarding disorder and other types of cluttering. You'll learn those differences in part 1.

It is important to recognize that possessions play a pivotal role in our daily lives. They say a lot about who we are, what we represent, what we do, and who we want to be. We often attach our fondest dreams and memories to our belongings. Like it or not, our possessions have power over our thoughts and emotions. However, when our items encroach on our living space and safety becomes an issue or the clutter interferes with our daily functioning, it's time to consider what we can do about it. It can be distressing to think about letting go of certain items or organizing your belongings, but if you want to reclaim your space, the strategies you'll learn in parts 2 and 3 can help you.

Because hoarding is highly stigmatized, many keep it a secret, not realizing that their problem is more common than they think. Researchers estimate that anywhere from 3 percent to 6 percent of the U.S. population struggles with some form of hoarding. This book relates the experiences of some of my clients (not identified by their real names). If your hoarding or cluttering feels debilitating, please seek professional advice. Recommendations for locating a professional are listed in the Resources section on page 150. This book is not a substitute for a mental health professional, and there is no shame in reaching out to a therapist and other professionals for help.

I commend you for picking up this book and taking this important first step. As you read, remember that you are not alone—there are others like you who struggle with clutter—and I'll be here, cheering you on. I hope you will use this book as a guide to understand and overcome the mental, emotional, and physical challenges of hoarding and cluttering and that you will gain the confidence to make lasting changes and learn strategies for reclaiming your life.

PART ONE

HOARDING 101

What is hoarding and how does it manifest? What are the differences between hoarding, cluttering, and collecting? Why do our possessions tend to play such a powerful role in our lives? Learning the answers to these questions is the first step to clearing your space.

1

What We Mean When We Talk about Hoarding

The way we make meaning of and organize our possessions varies from person to person, and for some of us, it becomes an issue. Despite all the storage bins, gadgets, and filing systems, clutter seems to be everywhere. Addressing this issue begins with understanding why you accumulate stuff.

In this chapter, we'll look at hoarding and its underlying causes. This topic can be difficult to discuss because there's a lot of misunderstanding and negativity associated with the terms *hoarder* and *hoarding*. Because *hoarder* can be used disparagingly, I encourage people to refrain from using it. Some prefer *clutterer*, *clutter bug*, and even *pack rat*. Whatever term we use, we need to approach the issue with compassion and empathy.

What Is Hoarding Disorder?

Hoarding disorder is a mental health diagnosis found in the *Diagnostic Statistical Manual of Mental Disorders*, 5th edition (*DSM-5*). The inclusion of the hoarding diagnosis in the go-to resource for mental health professionals is positive, because its presence there demonstrates the impact and prevalence of hoarding and allows clinicians to better help people with the disorder.

Hoarding disorder is defined as the persistent and chronic difficulty parting with possessions regardless of monetary value, accompanied by a strong urge or desire to save the items even if they are unusable at present. Difficulty discarding results in the accumulation of items that congest active living areas, such as the living room, kitchen, bedroom, and hallways, to the point where safety can be compromised. The hoarding behavior causes clinically significant distress that can complicate social, occupational, or other forms of functioning.

In defining the diagnostic criteria for hoarding disorder, the *DSM-5* points to features that may be present in those with hoarding disorder. First is the level of insight, or awareness, the person demonstrates regarding their hoarding problem:

> **Good or fair insight:** Awareness that a problem exists with one's hoarding-related beliefs and behaviors
> **Poor or absent insight:** Little to nonexistent awareness that a problem exists with one's hoarding-related beliefs and behaviors despite evidence to the contrary

Another feature to consider is excessive acquisition or the impulsive need to continue to acquire things even if there is no space in the home or even if the person is in debt. Sometimes people are not aware that they are struggling with this issue. We all hold on to things for a variety of reasons, which can be grouped into specific categories. These categories are the most common:

- **Sentimental:** Items that are kept as part of a memory or connection to an event or person, such as antiques, family photos and heirlooms, mementos from trips, and gifts and cards received over the years from close friends and loved ones

- **Intrinsic:** Possessions that have some sort of aesthetic value, for example, a piece of artwork, a decorative bowl, or an item in a favorite color

- **Instrumental:** Items that might serve a potential use in the future or come in handy one day, such as batteries, flashlights, and clothing

EXERCISE: FIVE REASONS YOU STILL HAVE IT

For all of the exercises in this book, I recommend that you keep a dedicated journal handy. Using a journal will allow you to keep the exercises in one place, do them as many times as you need (in as much space as you need), and reflect on how much progress you've made over the course of the book.

Now, think of just one item you have held on to for a long time. Grab your journal and write down the name of the item and list five reasons that contribute to your urge to hold on to it. This exercise helps you become aware. Let's say you are keeping a scarf because your best friend gave it to you years ago, but you never wear it. Your five reasons might be as follows:

1. I don't want to offend my friend by letting it go.

2. There isn't anything wrong with it—it's a perfectly good scarf!

3. I might need it as backup if I misplace my other scarves or one gets ruined.

4. I miss my friend, and this scarf brings back memories of her thoughtful ways.

5. I just love the fabric. Maybe I'll use it for a future quilting project!

Different Types of Hoarding/Cluttering

You're reading this book because you have excessive clutter and want to reduce what you have and organize what's left. You may not fit the diagnostic criteria of hoarding disorder but still have a big problem with clutter. So, what are the differences between chronic disorganization, hoarding behavior, and hoarding disorder? And what is squalor and what is animal hoarding? Let's explore what each of these terms actually means and how they might overlap.

CHRONIC DISORGANIZATION

Chronic disorganization refers to the countless attempts a person has made to try to organize their living spaces without success. The presence of clutter may be due to their difficulty organizing their belongings in a meaningful way. Although chronic disorganization can lead to cluttered living spaces and workspaces, it is not the same as hoarding disorder. People with chronic disorganization are generally agreeable to letting things go; they aren't rigid or strongly attached to a great number of possessions. Additionally, chronic disorganization may spill into other life areas, such as being chronically late for appointments or having trouble locating important items when needed. The terms *cluttering* and *chronic disorganization* are often used interchangeably. Chronic disorganization may be the result of attention-deficit/hyperactivity disorder (ADHD).

HOARDING BEHAVIOR

Hoarding behavior is not the same as hoarding disorder. Hoarding behavior can be present in other psychological or medical conditions, such as post-traumatic stress disorder (PTSD), ADHD, traumatic brain injury, social phobia, bipolar II disorder, eating disorders, substance abuse, and dementia. In fact, hoarding behavior can accompany any other medical condition or psychological disorder in much the same way depression can be present alongside other physical or mental health issues. For that reason, if the primary issue is treated, there may be improvements in the hoarding behavior.

SQUALOR

Although the words *squalor* and *hoarding* seem to run parallel with each other, they are not the same. Squalid, or unsanitary, home environments may suggest struggles with several different issues, such as self-neglecting behaviors or physical impairments/medical conditions that prohibit a person from cleaning. Squalor might also occur with other compounding mental health factors. Unfortunately, literature describing the causes of squalid home environments is lacking. What we do know is that the presence of squalor is rare among those who have hoarding disorder, but it can occur. Some people with hoarding disorder may live in unsanitary conditions as a consequence of severely cluttered spaces and/or poor planning and organizing. Squalor is almost always present in cases involving animal hoarding, discussed next.

ANIMAL HOARDING

Animal hoarding is when (1) a person keeps many animals or has more than the typical number of companion animals; (2) they struggle to provide the necessary conditions for a safe home, good nutrition, sanitation, and veterinary care for the animals; and (3) they continue to accumulate more animals despite having difficulty caring for their current animals. For more on this behavior, review the Hoarding of Animals Research Consortium (HARC) at Tufts University (see the Resources section, page 150). The American Society for the Prevention of Cruelty to Animals (ASPCA) offers support for this issue, as well.

OVERLAP IN TYPES OF HOARDING/CLUTTERING

Overlap between chronic disorganization, hoarding, and squalor can also exist. For instance, people who are chronically disorganized can demonstrate difficulty letting go of certain items. In those who struggle with hoarding, chronic disorganization can show up as distractibility, indecisiveness, disorganization, and categorization difficulties. As mentioned earlier, squalor can exist alongside or separate from other issues.

QUIZ: WHERE DO YOU FALL?

Read the following statements and identify those that resonate with you.

1. I often purchase replacement items because I lose track of what I already have.

2. I consistently run late to appointments and struggle to stay focused and on task because I can't keep track of my stuff (such as my keys and other items I need in the moment).

3. Past tips and tricks to achieve a more organized space haven't helped; keeping my belongings organized is a continuous struggle.

4. It's hard to address my clutter when I'm feeling mentally and/or physically fatigued; my clutter problem might be due to a mental health issue, such as depression, or a physical health issue.

5. I'm struggling to get a handle on my stuff, and I'm looking for ways to tackle the clutter.

6. I have strong attachments to most of my possessions.

7. I feel distressed when I think about making decisions regarding what to keep and what to let go of.

8. I don't invite people to my home because I don't want them to judge me or my place.

9. If I don't rescue another stray cat or adopt another dog from the shelter, one more animal will be without a forever home.

If statements 1, 2, and 3 resonate with you, you might be struggling with chronic disorganization. If statements 4 and 5 sound like you, you might be struggling with hoarding behavior. If you identify with statements 6, 7, and 8, you might be struggling with hoarding disorder. If statement 9 applies to you, you might be struggling with animal hoarding. And if some combination of those statements resonates with you, you might be struggling with more than one issue.

The Common Causes of Hoarding

Understanding causative factors can help you better understand why hoarding starts, which is valuable information for overcoming it. Let's take a look at these factors now.

TRIGGERING EVENTS

Hoarding disorder typically emerges during childhood or early adolescence. Children generally collect things, but their environments are controlled by adults, which makes hoarding behavior difficult to recognize. A child with hoarding issues may experience great distress if an item is taken away without their consent. Hoarding can be triggered by a variety of reasons, including a traumatic experience, stressful life events, perceived loss, grief, or bereavement.

Life transitions, such as retirement, loss of employment, divorce, periods of homelessness, serial moves, adult children leaving the home, and so on, can exacerbate hoarding. Stressful periods in life prompt different behaviors because everyone's journey is unique. So why do some people hoard and others don't? Sometimes insecurities and low self-esteem or even the absence of secure attachments as a child (that is, not feeling loved/nurtured by a parent) can spark hoarding behavior. Hoarding behavior provides a way to feel in control and to suppress emotional/psychological pain.

Real-Life Story

My client Lisa had a faint memory of hoarding behavior as a child following her parents' divorce and then the sudden passing of her father. She noticed over the years her strong desire to hold on to her belongings, including art projects, rocks and shells, clothing, and hair accessories. She told me her mother would clean up after her and try to throw out her "junk" when she wasn't around. These well-intentioned efforts didn't help the situation. Eventually, Lisa reached a point in her adult life at which her clutter interfered with her daily activities and social life. Through our work together, she connected her feelings of establishing control over her possessions as a way to control her life, which had seemed so out of control in her youth. By tackling her thought processes as well as her physical environment, Lisa started reducing clutter, which allowed her to meet her goal of inviting guests into her home.

BIOLOGY

Hoarding disorder may have a genetic component; most people with the disorder report having a close relative who is struggling with it. Studies have noted that more than three-quarters of people with hoarding disorder have at least one relative who had or has some sort of a hoarding problem.

SOCIETY

We live in a consumeristic society in which what we purchase can say a lot about who we are and maybe even how we would like to be perceived. Social meanings and values are therefore attributed to inanimate objects. We acquire things that are meaningful to us and often gift them to others. In this way, shopping is part of the social fabric of modern identity. Shopping can help those who hoard feel connected to the social world around them.

Researchers assert that there is a difference between people who have hoarding disorder and people who hold on to items due to their past experiences of scarcity. Hoarding is not a result of socioeconomic

Real-Life Story

While sorting with Nancy, I noticed that she had storage containers stacked inside of her pantry closet, tucked away in kitchen cabinets, and dispersed on the kitchen counters. She had an assortment of tops without bottoms and vice versa, so many of them were unusable. As we gathered all the containers, she contemplated her need to keep them. She told me that she grew up without much as a "Depression baby" and had to repurpose items, consume food (no matter what), and appreciate her belongings. It was clear from her stories that the sentiments she learned growing up transcended generations and influenced her decision-making, even in adulthood. Nancy took note of these ingrained lessons and how they had affected her, which enabled her to more clearly determine how many storage containers she actually needed.

background, and people who experience material scarcity in their life won't necessarily develop hoarding disorder. Indeed, hoarding can affect anyone—from those living below the poverty line to those living in affluent neighborhoods.

INGRAINED LESSONS

Ingrained lessons from childhood can have an impact on hoarding behavior. Statements we hear early on in life can make a lasting impression, especially repetitive *should* statements. An example of an ingrained lesson is "You should not be wasteful." This refrain is common among those who have experienced periods of financial or material insecurity. It can translate into routines like collecting bottles for the five-cent return (harmless) or into saving everything, creating a clutter problem.

MISPLACED INTENTIONS

For some people, acquisition helps minimize feelings of social isolation. I've had clients who purchased gifts for estranged family members only to never offer them because of fear of rejection. Keeping the gifts can subconsciously create the hope that the relationship will naturally mend. Other clients have kept items because they evoke memories of loved ones and good times. Again, the intention is to feel an emotional connection that an object cannot satisfy.

THE INFLUENCE OF OCD AND ADHD ON HOARDING

Many experts agree that hoarding disorder and obsessive-compulsive disorder (OCD) share many characteristics and that many people with hoarding disorder experience OCD as a co-occurring issue. So, how can we tell hoarding disorder and OCD apart? One of the most significant differences is the presence of both negative and positive emotions about belongings in hoarding disorder. The positive emotions (for example, admiration and desire) and negative emotions (for example, fear of societal pressure relating to hoarding) compete with each other and cause distress. People with OCD have predominately negative thoughts, which they attempt to neutralize through a series of compulsive behaviors.

Hoarding disorder is characterized by deficits in attention span, decision-making, organization, sorting, processing, and categorization. These deficits are also a feature of ADHD. But whereas people with ADHD can have difficulty discarding items because their decision-making is overwhelmed by external stimuli (for example, competing obligations and not knowing how to allocate their attention), people with hoarding disorder have that difficulty because their decision-making is overwhelmed by internal stimuli (thoughts).

Concentrating on specific tasks is a basic cognitive function that many people take for granted. Many factors can interrupt anyone's ability to focus. They include physical pain, depression, nervousness, and fatigue.

The Common Symptoms of Hoarding

People with hoarding disorder may regard their possessions as extensions of themselves, so much so that discarding them is akin to discarding some part of themselves. Likewise, they may regard throwing away items from loved ones as abandoning those loved ones.

One of my clients had a long-unused Christmas ornament she couldn't part with because it was a gift from her late sister. She explained that letting it go would be like throwing away her memory of her sister. She recognized the issue was created by her assignment of similar levels of importance to nearly everything she owned, but together we successfully challenged that way of thinking. Over time, a mug she'd bought when she was with her sister no longer held the same significance as the Christmas ornament.

In addition to valuing possessions as an extension of oneself or loved ones, common symptoms of hoarding can include the following:

- Attributing emotion to inanimate objects (anthropomorphizing)

- Significant distress when attempting to discard items, resulting in an inability to discard anything

- Difficulty categorizing and organizing possessions

- Indecision about what to keep and where to put kept items

- Embarrassment or shame about the state of one's home due to the multitude of possessions

- Wariness of having other people touch one's items

- Checking the trash for accidentally discarded objects

- Fear of running out of an item or believing one will need something in the future, even if they haven't used it in many years

- Social and physical impairments, such as diminished living spaces due to clutter, social isolation (fear of having people over), family or marital discord, financial difficulties (due to overspending and misplacing bills and checkbooks), and potential health hazards due to congested living areas

The Role of Excessive Acquisition in Hoarding

Purchasing and collecting items despite not having enough space or already owning similar items is known as excessive acquisition, which affects 80 to 90 percent of people with hoarding disorder. Stealing is less common; only 10 percent of people with hoarding disorder admit to stealing items. Chapter 5 discusses two means of acquisition: active acquisition, or intentional purchases, and passive acquisition, or the taking of free items.

The Common Traits of a Person Who Hoards

When it comes to hoarding disorder, no two people are the same, but compared with people who do not have the disorder, people who do have it typically have higher IQs, are more creative, attain higher levels of education, and experience greater levels of perfectionism. People I've worked with over the years are highly intelligent and consistently point out new ways to repurpose things I couldn't even begin to conceptualize. In general, people with hoarding disorder

- Hoard paperwork, clothing, and ungiven gifts to others

- Tend to be male

- Demonstrate difficulty making decisions, organizing, and categorizing belongings

- Have difficulty parting with belongings due to emotional attachments

- Tend to be socially isolated due to shame and embarrassment about the state of their homes and fear of judgment by others for the way they live

The Physical, Mental, and Emotional Components of Hoarding

Why do people hoard? This complicated question doesn't have a black-and-white answer according to the cognitive-behavioral model of hoarding, which attempts to explain the many variables that influence and sustain hoarding behavior. (A cognitive-behavioral model, in general, examines how people's thoughts or perceptions of situations influence their emotions and behavior.) This model includes information-processing deficits, emotional attachments, and unhelpful beliefs about possessions. Let's take a closer look.

INFORMATION-PROCESSING DEFICITS

Information-processing deficits are complications related to attention span, memory, categorization, and decision-making. For example, trying to stay focused on the task of sorting items can be difficult. However, in a cluttered home, there can be many competing demands for your attention. While trying to sort and organize, you might get distracted by something and find yourself walking away from your task. The thought of decluttering can feel overwhelming and even make you feel highly anxious, making it difficult to sort for longer than a few minutes. Organization and decision-making can be difficult because you may find yourself assigning each possession its own unique category, thereby making it impossible to meaningfully group items.

According to clinical trials, there are clear links between hoarding behavior and memory confidence as opposed to deficits with memory—meaning, the person doesn't trust their ability to remember where they place an item, so they will avoid putting it away in an appropriate location, such as a drawer, kitchen cabinet, or closet. Imagine someone has an important document in their hands and they want to make sure that it is kept in a place that is accessible and easy to remember. That location might be a dining table, so it is within sight. However, what happens when the next item also has that same level of importance? Important papers start to pile up on the table, eventually making it unusable for its intended purpose as a place to eat meals.

People with hoarding disorder also often exaggerate the importance of remembering things and believe that the only way to recall a particular experience is to hold on to a tangible item, a magazine or newspaper, for instance. Most people would find it impossible to remember every detail of something they've read, but people who hoard written materials often believe that they *should* be able to remember nearly everything. They can become increasingly frustrated by what they claim are "memory problems." The real problem is that they've set an unattainable standard for remembering, which is directly correlated with the high standards of perfectionism that those with hoarding disorder hold themselves to.

EMOTIONAL ATTACHMENTS

People who hoard typically form stronger attachments to their stuff than people who do not have this issue. The stuff becomes an intertwined part of themselves that represents personal histories and a reminder of distant memories. Because hoarding disorder is often connected to psychological trauma, loss, perceived loss, or significant life transitions (see page 9), rigidly holding on to items can serve as ways to make up for emotional loss over time. Sometimes accumulating stuff can be seen as a way to fill an emotional void. Whether acquired or saved, the possessions can provide moments of temporary relief from any emotional turmoil the person is experiencing.

UNHELPFUL BELIEFS ABOUT POSSESSIONS

People who hoard often feel overly responsible for their items and feel that they should always be prepared for different scenarios. This "just in case" way of thinking can result in the accumulation of excess supplies, like batteries, candles, containers, boxes, and so on. However, this feeling extends to a strong sense of responsibility for the well-being of an item itself. In a way, people who hoard believe they are safeguarding the items from harm, such as by ensuring that things are repurposed or recycled in a meaningful way. Also, if something is to be donated, that item must first be in pristine condition (for example, clothing should be laundered, ironed, folded, and presented carefully for drop-off); however, these very beliefs can stop items from reaching those who may be able to use them.

Effects on Loved Ones

Whether or not others live with the person who has hoarding disorder, the condition can often affect relationships. Loved ones may wonder why they are never invited to the person's home or may give a gift they never see the person use because it's been lost in their home. They may know that the person has a problem and may try to broach the subject, but their attempts at conversation are resisted, leaving them feeling frustrated and powerless to help. Interestingly, research shows that family members are more likely to seek professional guidance for their relative who hoards, but the person might refuse help or be in denial.

People who live in the same home as someone who hoards often report chronic headaches and respiratory issues. They are at an increased risk of falling due to the clutter and are also embarrassed to have workers or guests in the home. These issues can create a strong feeling of resentment toward the person who hoards. Children who grow up in homes where one or both parents hoarded may build life-long resentment toward their parents. This amount of resentment can lead to lifelong estranged relationships. (You'll find a few resources for children of parents who hoard in the Resources section, page 150.)

EXERCISE: CONVERSATION ABOUT CLUTTER

Think of the last time you had a conversation with a loved one about your clutter. How did that conversation go? Try to recall both the negative and positive points of that discussion, and write them in your journal.

If the conversation didn't go well and you could rewrite that conversation, how would it sound? What would they say and how would you respond, and vice versa? Jot down this ideal scenario in your journal. Now think more expansively: If that conversation really occurred that way, how would it benefit your relationship with that person?

When to See a Professional

If hoarding is negatively impacting your life and hindering your safety and the safety of those who live with you, including any pets in your home, it is important to explore professional help. Cognitive behavioral therapy (CBT), for example, entails behavior modification, learning to challenge erroneous beliefs, implementing skills and strategies (learning ways to sort and discard), work on maintenance, and setting up for the recovery journey, just to name a few components. A variety of mental health professionals provide CBT. These professionals can be helpful in treating underlying hoarding symptoms as well as co-occurring mental health issues, like depression and anxiety.

I recommend doing your research and putting together a list of questions you would like answered ahead of time. Start with a general search to locate an expert online (see the Resources section, page 150), consult your insurance company's directory of mental health providers, or ask your physician for referrals and recommendations. Remember that therapy is a dual process with goals that you and your therapist create together. If you are having difficulty expressing yourself in sessions or feel overwhelmed by your goals, speak to your therapist to see if you can work on this issue with them. If you are still having trouble communicating, you may need a different therapist. It can be difficult and painful to share your story more than once, but think about the long-term gains of finding the right therapist for you, and keep trying.

There Is Hope

The information in this chapter may be difficult to wrap your head around, especially if you are struggling with getting control of your clutter. The good news is that you've already come so far by opening this book, and this information will help you help yourself and others in your life who may be struggling. Therapy is a great option, but it is not the only option. There are many support groups available around the country (see the Resources section, page 150).

The narrative around hoarding is shifting and becoming more positive, which is wonderful. People are using language like *recovery* to describe combating hoarding symptoms, changing habits, and working toward maintaining success. Recovery is possible, change is possible, and we'll continue to explore ways to break down the barriers to success.

Conclusion

Hopefully you have a clearer understanding of what hoarding is. Perhaps you've recognized yourself in some of these descriptions or maybe you believe you don't have hoarding disorder but still struggle with clutter. Whatever the case may be, the beautiful thing to emphasize is that the narrative around this problem is changing, awareness is increasing, and people are coming together with hopeful language to help one another in their path toward recovery. We'll continue the conversation in the next chapter.

Self-Care Tip

A critical part of your decluttering journey is incorporating more self-care into your everyday life. Give yourself moments of wellness every day to reduce the possibility of burnout. Ideas include going for a walk, drinking more water, watching a movie, listening to music, or whatever brings you joy—even if it's only for a few minutes.

CHAPTER TWO

The People Who Hoard and Their Stuff

In this chapter, we'll explore some of the deeper motivations, behaviors, and rationales behind people's complications with clutter. We will also discuss how these complications are difficult to combat and how it can be easy to get stuck in the same mode of thinking as it pertains to our stuff. Being aware of all the intricacies involved in keeping you stuck can help you start to recognize your own behaviors, which will prepare you to change your tactics, tackle your clutter, and regain control.

The Differences between Cluttering, Collecting, and Hoarding Disorder

People have cluttering issues for a variety of reasons. With hoarding disorder, there are strong attachments to a great number of possessions, distress around the issue, and social impairments resulting from the volume of possessions. Someone who struggles with a cluttering problem may not exhibit the same level of attachment or distress as someone who has hoarding disorder. Visually, their home looks cluttered due to various other reasons, like not having enough time to tend to the stuff, getting easily distracted, or just overall difficulty managing an organized space and lifestyle.

There are also collectors, who have many items on display but may have neither a hoarding problem nor a problem with organization. Both collectors and people who hoard value their collections. A distinguishing factor is the way the collectables are displayed and the number of collections. A collector displays their items in an organized fashion and spends time and energy maintaining the collection. Collections become problematic only if they negatively encroach on the space and impact the way that space is intended to be used.

EXERCISE: HOW DO YOU IDENTIFY?

Read these three descriptions and choose the one that best describes you:

- **I'm a collector:** There is some rhyme and reason to the items I collect. My collections are limited to certain categories, such as baseball cards, coins, or figurines. I display my collections or keep them in such a manner that I can easily share them with people who are interested in seeing them.

- **I'm a clutterer:** I have some attachment to my possessions, like anyone else, but mainly my home just seems to always be disorganized. Whenever I try to organize, I get pulled in different directions; I feel like I don't have the time to straighten up, or I get distracted by other people or tasks that demand my attention.
- **I think I might have a hoarding problem:** The number of possessions I have makes it difficult for me to fully utilize all the rooms in my home. I feel emotionally distressed by the volume of items in my home; therefore, I experience some sort of impairment in my life, such as in my daily routines, social activities, family gatherings, or financial complications due to acquiring.

A Cluttering Problem Is Not Hoarding Disorder

Just because a person has excessive clutter in their home does not necessarily mean that they will develop hoarding disorder. As you have learned, hoarding disorder is a mental health diagnosis, and certain beliefs and behaviors must be present. In the previous chapter, we discussed the different types of hoarding and cluttering. Yes, there may be some overlapping qualities of incessant accumulation and collections of items. For some, the propensity to collect things is a way to relieve anxiety. However, with hoarding disorder, the clutter creates safety concerns and generates strong levels of distress for the person. Additionally, with hoarding disorder, the person displays strong attachments to nearly every item, which is accompanied by anxiety at the thought of letting it go. These markers are what differentiates cluttering from hoarding disorder.

Real-Life Story

My client Ed came across a recipe for a drink he enjoyed when he was in college, 40 years earlier. Holding up the aged notecard, he shared how he and his friend used to make this delicious and deceptively strong alcoholic drink. He said he wanted to keep it just in case he ever felt ambitious enough to make it again, even though he admitted that one of the main ingredients was no longer easy to find. He vacillated over whether or not to keep the recipe. He rationalized keeping it by saying it was just a small piece of paper and maybe he would pass it on to his nephew. In the process, one of his fears came to the surface: If he let the recipe go, he might forget all the wonderful memories of his youth. This example shows how things can become woven into the fabric of a person's life. Ed set aside the recipe temporarily, and when we revisited it next, he realized that the drink is very high in sugar and he would never make it again. He decided to discard it.

Why Do We Let Stuff Rule Us?

The common chatter around hoarding and cluttering is that it is all about control, but if the personal need for control is such a big part of this phenomenon, why do people wind up feeling controlled by their possessions? My client Rick once said that he felt like his home was possessing him instead of the other way around, and he desperately wanted to flip the script. Attempts to "control" stuff can serve as an unconscious function to feel connected with the world and remain relevant. Clipped coupons, notes on scrap paper, various magazine articles (or the magazines themselves), excess storage containers, and the like are all kept with the intention of passing them on to someone who might need or want them someday, even if the recipient is not initially identified.

BIOLOGY

Basic biological requirements (also known as physiological needs) are things we all need to survive and thrive in our environments. Such biological needs are air, food, drink, shelter, clothing, and warmth. According to a motivational theory in psychology known as Maslow's hierarchy of needs, physiological needs must be met before we are motivated to pursue higher-level needs. Often, when cluttering exists, the need to satisfy basic biological needs can be exaggerated. People who hoard understand they need food, water, and clothing but may take this need to an extreme by amassing an overabundance of such things. Some who are in severe situations, where they reach a point of crisis and face threats of potential eviction or condemnation of their property, may overfocus on other important issues instead of working to reduce their clutter to preserve their housing. In these examples, hoarding is not necessarily a result of people confusing their priorities but can be a consequence of the underlying mental issue itself.

SOCIETY

The history of consumerism can provide us with context regarding attitudes and beliefs about possessions and our need to acquire more stuff. Shopping has generated a culture that can be used by anyone regardless of class background to generate social prestige through fashionable trends and brands. In the 1950s, sociologist Georg Simmel described fashion as the means by which people express themselves and generate social ties with the world around them. So it is no wonder that what we own presents the version of ourselves we want to portray to our extended social circles—for example, "I am financially stable because I can afford that," "I am smart because I got this item at a bargain price," or "I can share my secrets of locating great buys at exceptional locations."

Society also gives us the impression that our stuff will make life easier. We're led to believe that good old retail therapy will solve everything. People who hoard can experience extended periods of emotional distress, limited social exposure, and feelings of shame and embarrassment while also struggling with core emotional burdens, like loss and grief. Having stuff and buying stuff not only produce momentary glimpses of distraction from these tough experiences but also serve as an invisible cape where the person is trying to say, "I'm fine."

COMPULSION AND THE NEED TO SAVE

A constant denominator in hoarding is the perceived need to save virtually anything and everything. The driving factor is that the person sees value and purpose in the saved items, whether sentimental, intrinsic, and/or instrumental (see pages 4–5). However, they have difficulty organizing the items in a meaningful way. This disorganization can look like a scrap envelope with notes written on the back, a ripped-out piece of paper that has phone numbers on it without a name listed, or a broken porcelain coffee creamer (that could be repaired and used or displayed as a decorative item). There are varied reasons for what should be saved, what should be repaired, what should be a new hobby, and what should be followed up on. Whether or not we have a cluttering problem, these considerations are common. So, what makes saving things a problem? The issue is not the nature of individual attachments but rather the expansive net that is cast over a host of items and the intensity attributed to the need to save them all.

THE FEAR OF WASTE

The need to save things often centers on avoiding waste, even if the items seem to have no apparent use or purpose. People who hoard may have ingrained fears about waste that are reminiscent of the scrupulosity obsessions that are sometimes seen in those with OCD. Scrupulosity obsessions are characterized by guilt or obsessional thoughts associated with religious or moral issues that result in compulsive behaviors, such as excessive confessions and seeking repetitive reassurance from spiritual leaders to avoid the possibility of sinning. A similar concept presented in hoarding disorder has been coined *material scrupulosity*. It is an exaggerated sense of moral or ethical duty to avoid waste at any cost and with great care for the disposition of items in such a way that they can be reused.

Real-Life Story

The extent to which my client Marta would go to recycle and avoid discarding things was remarkable. She expressed that she should wash everything and make sure that it is recycled because "it is the right thing to do." What struck me was the "should" statement. She *should* do this process properly but according to whom? When I asked this question, she said it was something she had always done; it was the right thing to do. It was later revealed that she attended parochial school as a child and was raised in a devout Roman Catholic family. "The nuns told me that it is a sin to waste," she said with a snicker. She struggled with material scrupulosity.

The extent to which Marta avoided waste hindered her life. She saved everything (whether or not she wanted it) because of her ingrained belief that it was a sin to waste anything. She would wash out empty peanut butter jars and soak the labels off prescription bottles to ready them for recycling. She would then let these things accumulate, but she couldn't just throw them away. Marta eventually learned to refocus her waste avoidance on sorting and organizing.

SHAME SPIRALS

Shame is arguably one of the most destructive emotions we can experience. Shame can be described as that painful, deteriorating feeling that tricks our minds into thinking we are not worthy, there is something wrong with us, or we are defective in some way. Sometimes, the critical words people say to us can really stay with us—after all, we aren't made with a nonstick coating! Rejection or negative comments by friends can lead to feelings of shame that snowball into larger problems. People with hoarding disorder, anxiety, depression, and other issues can spend time repeatedly ruminating on these negative dialogues, even to the point of never expecting to hear a validating comment from others. For many, a way to distract themselves from spiraling shame is to enjoy certain possessions or buy new items.

DEALS AND STEALS

There is a store here in New England where people can donate their once-loved treasures, and a portion of the proceeds goes to benefit a local charity. Many of my clients know this place by name because it has bargains that are "too good to pass up." Virtually everyone has a store that is too irresistible to pass by without walking in and feeling the need to purchase something. These places are what I call high-trigger locations. Stores in this category can be thrift shops, hardware stores, office suppliers, craft stores, and so on. The high-trigger locations are based on individual preferences, and when there's a sale, it feels too difficult to resist. Sometimes, it's not a store at all; people can be drawn in by yard sales, flea markets, or free items on the side of the road, all in pursuit of a good deal. (There's more on high-trigger locations in chapter 5.)

CONTROL

The feeling of control is a common theme with regard to acquiring and cluttering. When helpers try to take charge, a person can feel that their autonomy is being threatened. Decisions regarding wanting to save things and acquiring more can get confused with maladaptive beliefs regarding control and independence. We need to be able to distinguish between when our choices are healthy and when they can be self-damaging. For example, sometimes people want to do the exact opposite of what their family members tell them to do, which may lead to not making progress on their personal goals. It is important to be aware of this potential reaction and adjust when moments of defiance are creating stagnation.

REMINDERS OF OUR PAST

The things we collect in our homes often have sentimental value—family photos, mementos from travels abroad, gifts from loved ones, belongings from family members who are no longer with us. We all have those treasured items that hold some of our fondest memories. When everything has sentimental value (a grandparent's dining set, for instance, even though you already have your parents' dining set), reminders of the past can begin piling up. Giving away possessions that were once owned by close loved ones is very difficult. Sometimes, keeping the items helps the person feel close to those who are no longer with them, and letting go of the items means that the person really is no longer here.

EXERCISE: WHY CAN'T YOU LIVE WITHOUT IT?

Pick an object in your home that you hold in high regard. You may have many that are highly important to you, but try to choose just one. Think for a moment about why this item means so much to you. Think about the ways you have come to love it. In your journal, write all the ways you believe this object is important to you and why you feel that you can't live without it. Again, this exercise is designed to help you become more aware of your relationship with your belongings.

INSECURITIES

For many people who have a cluttering problem, their possessions become extensions of their identities and serve as reminders of who they are in the world, the parts of themselves they feel secure about. An example is someone who wants to hold on to all their business attire even though they are now retired. Keeping these possessions provides tangible evidence of their high-powered career in which they felt important and respected. One of my clients struggled to let his professional wardrobe go for this reason. He was concerned that if he got rid of these clothes, there would be nothing left of him. In other cases, people hold on to things because they reflect their aspirations of who they want to be or how they want to be perceived in this world.

Perfectionism is also an issue related to insecurity. What makes perfectionism consequential is that the desire for success is only a response to avoiding failure. There are overlapping themes between shame and perfectionism as ways to navigate around harsh judgment and criticism. Someone who struggles with clutter may avoid taking steps to sort and organize because they anticipate someone else will say their efforts weren't good enough.

Real-Life Story

My client Jack had a specific object he wanted to discuss with me: a candle holder his father had given him as a housewarming gift. He never used it but could never bear to part with it. He said he hadn't seen it in years because it was buried among other items in his home. Being faced with the object after all these years, he said he was flooded with negative thoughts and memories of his abusive childhood. He announced that he wanted to dispose of it. He planned to throw it away outside in his trash barrel. He looked at me with his eyes shining with tears and declared he was ready. He reported that he wanted to throw it away, and so he did. His exuberant strength was displayed, and our ears caught the loud and contained crashing of the metal inside of the barrel.

SAFETY

Themes of safety and security often come up in my work with clutter. The abundance of clutter in a home can create safety concerns if pathways are obstructed or if things are piled so high that's there's a potential for an avalanche, but paradoxically, people with clutter and hoarding issues often amass things to feel secure. Some clients have informed me that without all the stuff, they would actually feel less safe. Unfortunately, some of my clients report having been attacked in their homes by intruders or abusive family members. For them, the hoarding behaviors increased as a way for them to feel in control and more secure. These clients disclose feeling that their piles of treasures prohibit the potential for a repeat attack to occur, which speaks to the relevance of the role of psychological trauma in hoarding behavior. If you resonate with this feeling, consider your next steps on your path toward healing. People heal from trauma in several ways. What remains constant is the need for courage, strength, and perseverance. See the Resources section (page 150) for helpful websites.

Begin to Take Control

Accumulating things over the years may have subconsciously served as a way for you to feel in control. However, you may have come to the realization that clutter is actually controlling you and your decisions. Without feeling a sense of agency, people can develop a sense of passivity and helplessness, which can lead to mental and physical health complications. One way to regain control is to ask for help. Another way is to take time for self-care, and each chapter concludes with a self-care tip to help you on your way. Other ways of taking charge include saying no to things that are not priorities. Your happiness, your safety, and your mental and physical well-being are priorities. By reading this book, you are taking an initial step toward doing things differently and putting yourself first.

No matter how long you have been struggling with clutter, you do have the power to regain hold over your emotions, thoughts, behaviors, and possessions. However, overcoming hoarding behavior is a process; you will have periods of doubt and periods of success. Have patience with yourself. With patience and effort, you can eventually take full control.

Conclusion

As you've learned, there is much more to the problem of hoarding and cluttering than meets the eye. You've had a good overview of the factors at play, and perhaps you've resonated with these discussions. As you move on to part 2, think about how your life will be changed by your decision to move toward a clutter-free life. Consider the ways in which avoidance and excuse-making have held you back, and ponder the actions you can take that will lead to better results. The next part of the book will prepare you for success with strategies and exercises to help you figure out your next steps.

Self-Care Tip

Treat yourself to an activity that brings you joy and doesn't involve shopping or acquiring items. Go out for lunch, stroll through a park, take the dog for a walk, or read a book or article that has been on your must-read list.

PART TWO

STRATEGIES FOR MENTAL AND EMOTIONAL PREPARATION

In this part of the book, you'll learn some strategies to assist you in developing your personal goals for tackling clutter as well as how to prioritize these goals. First, you'll find some suggestions for physically handling your belongings with the right mindset. Then you'll learn some ways to boost your motivation while working on the clutter to achieve your goals.

CHAPTER THREE

Prioritize Your Goals

Now that you have a better understanding of the complexities behind the clutter, it's time to identify and learn how to prioritize your goals. But let's pause here so I can commend you for all the hard work you've already done to combat this problem. It's okay if you feel like the work you have dedicated toward the improvement of your living space hasn't quite paid off. This book is here to help. Let's begin by setting the stage for the future you envision.

Setting the Stage

Think about the goals you would like to set for yourself. Maybe you want a clear space, a more organized life, and a way to bring your shopping habits into check. These long-term goals are all fantastic, but they are very general. You'll need to find a way to break your goals down into specific, measurable actions. The following exercise can help you clarify your long-term vision for different aspects of your life and keep you motivated for the duration of our work together and beyond.

EXERCISE: FIVE-MINUTE VISUALIZATION

Go somewhere you won't be disturbed. Sit in a comfortable position and have your journal handy. Set a timer for five minutes and close your eyes.

1. Imagine that while you are sleeping tonight peacefully in your quiet home, a *miracle* occurs: Your problem with clutter is solved. Every distraction, the number of possessions, your difficulties with attachments, excessive shopping habits, debt, and/or complicated relationships are all resolved! When you wake up in the morning, your home is just the way you want it to be. How is your life different now? (Not how is your *home* different, but how is your *life* different?) Continue to envision this scenario until the timer goes off.

2. Open your eyes and describe your experience in your journal. How did it feel to visualize your life without the clutter?

3. Now turn your attention back to your present circumstances and answer the following questions:

   - What is the clutter in your home keeping you from doing even though you want to be able to do those things?
   - What steps do you need to take to gain control over the clutter so that your life can be the way you envisioned it?

- What would be the first small sign that tells you that you are gaining control over the clutter? (Perhaps trying one of the strategies in this book!)

Strategies for Setting Your Priorities and Sorting Goals

Here are some action steps you can take to start setting specific goals and getting your priorities in order. Setting priorities applies to what actually happens before, during, and after your sorting sessions.

1. RATE YOUR SPACE

The clutter image rating (CIR) scale is a pictorial assessment tool that allows you to recognize your level of clutter by assigning a rating of 1 to 9 to your room based on the volume of items compared to nine photographs with increasing levels of clutter. You can easily find the CIR scale online if you type "clutter image rating" into your Internet browser. As you'll see from the images, a rating of 1 means that there is virtually no clutter within the room. A rating of 9 means there is a great deal of clutter. This scale is not intended as a diagnostic tool; however, ratings from 4 to 9 suggest difficulty with clutter.

Images are a powerful way to generate an objective view of your home. By bringing you back to an objective reality, photographs can help you generate goals. By using the rating scale, much of the subjectivity is eliminated because you are simply assigning a number corresponding to the level of clutter per each room. The CIR scale is helpful in establishing a baseline of how you rate the clutter today and how you would like to rate each room. As you move on, you can reassess to measure your progress. For example, your baseline might be 7. Then two weeks later, you notice it went down to a 6. Getting into the habit of taking before-and-after photos of your space will help you achieve your goals in the long run.

Looking at the CIR scale, assign a rating to each area of your home in your journal:

- Basement
- Bathroom(s)
- Bedroom #1
- Bedroom #2

- Dining room
- Garage
- Hallway, main
- Hallways, other

- Kitchen
- Living room
- Yard, back
- Yard, front

2. IDENTIFY A TARGET ROOM AND SELECT ONE AREA

Select a room you would like to work on first—your target room. Knowing you will be working in this one room rather than jumping around from room to room will help you focus your attention and efforts in that space, making it easier to see your progress. Recognizing your progress and what you've accomplished goes a long way toward keeping you motivated, which we will discuss more in chapter 4. Your progress is more difficult to notice if you tackle many rooms at once.

In your journal, jot down the target room you would like to start on. Perhaps you've selected your kitchen, dining room, main hallway, living room, or bedroom. It's up to you where to start. (In chapter 7, we'll discuss a room-by-room task list.) For now, simply select the target room. Spend a few moments thinking about why you selected this room.

Think of the target room in terms of specific areas to make the idea more manageable. For example, if you chose your kitchen, break down the room into countertops, kitchen table, lower cabinets, upper cabinets, pantry closet, and so on. Plan to tackle a specific area and keep building from there. Doorways and windows are good places to start to make those areas accessible and increase safety in your home.

3. CREATE SORTING CATEGORIES

Sorting precedes organization. As a first step, you need to sort your belongings. But before you begin sorting in your target area, you will need to create a system that can help you achieve success. Some people like boxes, bins, or even bags. Whichever you choose, you need to create structure to help you with decision-making. Having a limited number of categories is critical; too many categories will make it more difficult to meaningfully organize your possessions. Label your sorting containers as follows:

- Keep

- Donate

- Discard

If it takes longer than 15 seconds to make a decision, put the item aside temporarily (see page 50). If you have a lot of recycling (paper, plastic, and glass), you can add a "recycle" container.

4. LEARN THE OHIO RULE

"OHIO" is a common rule in the clutter-helping world. OHIO stands for "only handle it once" (or at most twice). The idea is not to have more than one item in your hand at a time. Pick up a single item, place it in its container (keep, donate, or discard), and then move on to the next item. Avoid holding items in your left hand while picking up something else with your right. Decide the category for each item before picking up the next one.

5. SET SMART GOALS

Setting SMART (specific, measurable, attainable, relevant, and time-bound) goals helps you identify specific, concrete objectives. Using this approach helps change the task from "clean up the entire room" to "sort half of the dining table today." Set SMART goals for your sorting sessions as well as SMART goals for yourself each week. What can you commit to for the week? What is the probability you will be able to complete your goals for the week? Sample SMART goals for the week might include "Donate two bags of clothing to the clothing drop-off bin this week," "Recycle four newspapers each week," or "Sort through one bin of winter clothing on Monday."

Remember to evaluate the accomplishment of your SMART goals (in your journal) at the time you specified. Were you able to accomplish your SMART goals for your session or for the week? How would you rate your accomplishment on a scale of 0 to 10, and why? If you feel your rating is too low, adjust your SMART goals so they are more attainable.

EXERCISE: YOUR TOP 10 GOALS FOR YOUR TARGET ROOM

Think about you, your journey, and your personal goals. Do not think about goals that are driven by family members and others. What do you want for yourself? Think about what you hope to accomplish along this journey and how you would like your space to look. Once you have selected your target room, write down your top 10 goals for this space in your journal. Be imaginative. For example, your top 10 goals for your kitchen may be as follows:

1. To have clear countertops on which you can prepare your food

2. To access your cooking utensils with ease

3. To have designated space for your serving dishes and plates

4. To eat meals at your kitchen table

5. To grow herbs on the kitchen windowsill

6. To set up your coffee maker in a little coffee nook

7. To have all your paper goods, like napkins and paper plates, on one shelf

8. To have a designated cabinet for food storage containers and plastic baggies

9. To have a designated pantry for canned and boxed goods

10. To cook your favorite recipes again

6. CREATE A SCHEDULE AND SORT DAILY

This journey is about establishing new habits. Scheduling 30 minutes to sort daily helps you generate a new routine, and because you do a little each day, you will be minimizing your chances of burnout. You can have more than one 30-minute sorting session a day, but remember, you are not running a marathon. Scheduling one or two 30-minute sorting sessions each day will help you grow accustomed to developing your sorting muscle and feeling comfortable around the process. The more you practice sorting using the strategies in this book, the more your awareness of your emotions, thoughts, and behaviors will grow.

Pencil in your sorting session like a routine appointment. If daily sorting is just not doable due to your obligations and responsibilities, schedule your sessions every other day. When I work with clients, we always talk this part out to arrive at what works best. It's important to work regularly on this. Try not to get too caught up on the strictness of the process, but do make sure you are carving out time to put in the work. Here is where accountability comes into play: You are embarking on a commitment to yourself to work on reducing the clutter.

7. SET A TIMER AND KEEP IT CLOSE

When you start your sorting session, set a timer for sorting. The previous strategy suggests 30 minutes, which may seem daunting, and that's okay! Start out with 10 minutes and build your way up. After a few sessions, go for 15, then 20, and then 30.

A timer is a good way to develop your sorting muscle and helps you avoid the inevitable burnout of "never-ending" sorting sessions. Maybe you think that if you dedicate eight straight hours or more, you can tackle the entire target room. I want you to pull yourself out of that type of thinking. A full day of sorting can lead to many days of avoiding sorting altogether because the all-day session took so much energy and effort. Give the timed sessions a chance.

While sorting, keep the timer next to you. Sorting can take a lot of your focus, and if you wander into another room, you might not hear the timer (but see the next strategy). Prior to starting the timer, think about your goals for the session (and write down these goals in your journal). When the timer goes off, think aloud (see page 48). Did you accomplish what you set out to do, or were you distracted? Which categories did you place the items into? Are you keeping most of the items?

8. SORT ONLY IN YOUR TARGET AREA

When you're working on sorting items in your target area, remain in the target area. In other words, try not to leave the area to put things away in other areas of the home or room. Instead, use your sorting categories. You can put the items away later. Leaving your target area during your sorting exercise can lead to distractions, which I've seen happen many times. Someone will say, "I'll just put it away right over here," but then their attention gets directed elsewhere. So stay in the same place until you are finished with your sorting for the session.

9. PRESS THE EASY BUTTON

A common mistake people make with sorting is starting with some of the more difficult categories or items to make decisions about. When I say "difficult," I am referring to items that trigger the most attachment, emotions, meanings, and thoughts that keep you stuck. Some examples might be family photos, greeting cards, and clothing from a family member who has passed on. Sometimes paperwork can be difficult because of all the reading/skimming that needs to occur before deciding what to do with each piece of paper.

Instead, I want you to think about a concept I use called the "easy button." This concept refers to things that are less difficult for you to sort. As with weight lifting, you need to build yourself up by increasing your strength before adding more weight. In other words, you need to start off a little lighter to make this process tolerable and manageable. So, go ahead and press your easy button.

EXERCISE: WHAT'S YOUR EASY BUTTON?

This exercise helps you become aware of why you are less attached to some items than you are to others. It also helps you examine your reasons for keeping certain belongings. I'm encouraging you not to throw anything away but just to become aware of your thoughts and feelings. In your journal, write your responses to the following prompts:

- Select three items from your target room: (1) one thing that is easy to let go of, (2) one thing that would be moderately difficult to let go of, and (3) one thing that would be incredibly difficult to let go of. Write these three items down, and label them "easy," "moderately difficult," and "extremely difficult."
- Now, think about each of these items. What feelings come up for you with each item? Does thinking about the item bring up feelings of happiness, sadness, anger, excitement, or something else?
- What thoughts came up for you about each item? Some examples include "I must keep this—it's my favorite," "I forgot I had this," "I have been looking for this!" and "I'm not sure why I've kept this."
- What action did you take with each item? Did you decide to let any of the items go? If so, which ones and why? Or did you put the items back where they came from or put them somewhere else?

What did you notice about yourself during this exercise? Did you find yourself getting overwhelmed or distracted? Increased awareness helps you begin to identify and change unhelpful thoughts and behaviors.

10. NOTICE YOUR THOUGHTS AND FEELINGS

Our thoughts and emotions often dictate our behaviors and the actions we take. To generate new habits and allow for those new habits to stick, start paying critical attention to your thought patterns. When it comes to sorting, some common inner dialogue might sound like "I'm afraid to sort because I don't have enough time to do it all," or "I don't want to sort because I might make a mistake by getting rid of something I cannot replace." Statements along these lines can cause stagnation because they don't move you forward.

You have the power to take control of your thoughts and take action toward your goals. Taking back control starts by becoming aware. As you begin sorting the items in your target area, pay attention to the following:

- How are you feeling (e.g., anxious, scared, tired, overwhelmed, happy, excited, angry, or something else)?

- What are you thinking (e.g., *I am so close to kicking this habit! Where do I begin? When will I ever get this place cleared up? I want to stop sorting for right now and I'll get back to it another time.*)?

- What are you doing? (e.g., placing items in the labeled containers, thinking too much about each item, moving items from one area into another, undesignated area)?

11. THINK ALOUD AS YOU SORT

We think all the time, sometimes without being aware of what we're thinking. To start recognizing your thoughts, practice thinking aloud as you sort. Here's how:

1. Pick up an item and name it aloud.

2. Describe what you like about the item (color, texture, utility, etc.).

3. Describe what you do not like about the item (size, needs repair, etc.).

4. What would you use it for? When?

5. When is the last time you used it?

6. Are you realistically going to use it again?

7. Where should it go (where is its *home*, as I like to call it)?

8. Which sorting category does it fall into?

Real-Life Story

After Maureen and I had been working together for some time, she reached a point at which she wanted to sort through her books. While sorting books into the "keep" and "donate" categories, she questioned what she really liked about each book. She noticed how her preferences have shifted over the years. She asked herself, "Will I really ever read this?" and tested herself when she encountered books she thought she would read but hadn't. She limited her "keep" pile to the books she knew she would try to read for self-care. She felt good about being able to donate her books to others who could appreciate her treasures.

12. MINIMIZE DISTRACTIONS

Everyone gets distracted by different stimuli. Having the television on while you sort is an obvious distraction because it will draw your attention in as it is designed to do. Some people like to work in the quiet and find it helpful, but others may find silence a distraction. What is your preference? If silence can be distracting for you, turn on soothing music (like classical music), but don't have the volume up so high that it will interfere with your think-aloud process. Likewise, if you play songs with lyrics, you might find yourself singing along with the songs, which will also interfere with thinking out loud.

13. PUT IT ASIDE TEMPORARILY

While you are sorting, if you come across a distressing item that might stop you in your tracks, try the following:

- Hold and describe the item.

- What emotions are you experiencing as you hold and describe this item?

- If your emotions were in charge, what would they tell you to do? Would they tell you to stop sorting because you are feeling too anxious to continue?

- If you were in charge, what would you tell yourself? Would you tell yourself to keep your goal in mind and continue working? Would you remind yourself that with forward movement, you will feel better?

Once you're done, go ahead and put the item aside if you are still not ready to address it, and continue sorting through the other items. This way you can keep moving forward. I'll discuss using this and similar strategies more in the upcoming chapters.

EXERCISE: NEED VERSUS WANT

Sometimes we hold on to an item because we want it, and other times we keep it because we feel we need it. What are some things we absolutely cannot live without? Some of our basic needs include health, fresh air, housing, food, and water. How can you distinguish needs from wants? Wants are things we could live without and still survive. As you sort, think aloud in terms of need versus want: Pick up an item and ask yourself, "Is this satisfying a need or a want?" Think about what would happen if you elected to let go of it. If it is something you could survive without, it's a want rather than a need. If you want it, that's okay, of course. Just start becoming aware of the difference between *need* and *want*.

14. WHEN YOUR SESSION ENDS

Once you have come to the end of your sorting session, put away things in your "keep" category: Identify homes for the items where you can easily and safely access them at this point. It's fine if this step isn't possible at this stage of your journey. Some people I've worked with over the years weren't able to access those homes until all the sorting was complete. In that case, just make sure that the container in which your "keep" items reside is clearly labeled. Doing so will keep you from sorting through those items again at a later date.

Donate the items in your "donate" container as soon as possible. Identify a place that accepts donations and then get those giveaway items out of your home. Try to refrain from waiting until you have a "big enough" pile to donate. Seeing the things that you decided to part with leave your home will help you notice your progress and keep up the momentum.

Let go of the items in your "discard" pile. Now that you have made the decision to discard those items, see it through and let them go. Once items have been placed in the rubbish barrels or recycling bins, trust the reason you decided to let go and try to refrain from retrieving them.

15. CREATE A STAGING AREA

If you can't access the appropriate homes for your "keep" items yet, you may need a "staging area" for those items. Here, you will group similar items together in labeled bins and boxes. I've created staging areas many times with clients but especially in highly cluttered homes. I once worked with a family who blocked off a room for their staging area with bins and boxes labeled *Christmas, picture frames, photos, decorations, clothing,* and so on. At the end of your sorting session, place each "keep" item into its respective category.

10 Decision-Making Questions to Ask Yourself

As you get used to sorting and thinking aloud, ask yourself these questions and state your answers aloud:

1. How many of this item do you already have? Is that enough?

2. Do you have enough time to use, review, and read written material, like books, newspapers, magazines, and pamphlets? If so, when?

3. Have you used the item in the past year? If not, what is the likelihood you will use this item again?

4. Do you have a specific plan for this item? By when?

5. Is this item important only because you are looking at it now?

6. If you didn't already own it, would you buy it again?

7. Is the item current, reliable, accurate, and in good condition?

8. Do you really need it? If you really needed it, could you get it again?

9. Do you have enough space for it? If, so where do you envision it going?

10. If it is important to you, how can you display it in a way that aligns with your preferences?

Conclusion

In this chapter, you've learned a number of strategies that can help you begin the sorting process with clear goals in mind. You are mentally prepared to start working toward your goals for your home—one target area at a time in incremental steps. In the next chapter, we'll look into some mental roadblocks that can hamper your motivation, and I'll offer you a number of strategies to get you back on track toward tackling the clutter.

Self-Care Tip

Spend time enjoying the fresh air. Go outside and appreciate the beauty and the scenery around you. Even if you don't live in an area with a lot of greenery, the sky is always an awesome sight. As you stand outside, just breathe. With each inhale, think of your newfound journey of taking your life back from your clutter. With each exhale, breathe out the fears and negative thoughts around your clutter, letting those worries and unhelpful thoughts drift away into the atmosphere. You got this!

CHAPTER FOUR

Boost Your Motivation

Motivation is the readiness to actively engage in reaching your desired goals. Maybe you are feeling very motivated right now—great! However, it's not uncommon for motivation to shift up and down, or "wax and wane." Motivation can even vary throughout the day. Struggles with motivation aren't unique to those with cluttering issues, of course. This chapter includes strategies to help you increase your motivation and sustain it with regard to tackling your clutter. I'll target saving behaviors, ways to resist acquiring, and how to identify negative thoughts that keep you at a standstill. We'll also take a close look at how to apply motivational techniques toward achieving your goals and living by your values.

What's Hindered Your Motivation in the Past?

It's likely you've tried to tackle your clutter in the past, and although you perhaps made some headway, something seemed to block you from moving forward. Do you know what got in the way of your progress? If you haven't tried to tackle your clutter before, this question still applies to you; something is blocking your way forward. I always find this question intriguing, and I think it's an important one to ask. Take a moment now to think over your journey thus far in the following exercise.

EXERCISE: WHEN DID CLUTTER BECOME A PROBLEM?

In your journal, respond to the following questions:

- When did you first notice that clutter was a problem for you? Did you recognize it yourself or did someone point it out to you?
- When was the first time you noticed negative consequences associated with this problem?
- When did you first start tackling this problem?
- How long have you spent working on this issue?
- Have you experienced any successful attempts at challenging this problem?
- If you've made progress in the past, what kept you from continuing?
- If you've made no progress or have not previously tried to tackle this issue, what got in the way?

Sometimes external factors, such as criticism from others who don't notice your hard work, keep you from feeling motivated. Internal reasons—getting distracted, putting yourself down, feeling tired, having chronic pain, or being depressed—may also get in the way. Perfectionism can play a role, too. I've noticed that people who struggle with perfectionism often find it challenging to accomplish their short- and long-term goals. If they can't do something completely or perfectly (that is, meet the high standards they've set for themselves), they might feel it's better to just put it off "for now."

How about you? Are your standards leading to procrastination? As you're sorting things, do you have thoughts like "I'll never get through it all," "My home will never get organized," or "When am I ever going to get a handle on all of this?" Maybe you can shake them off and continue sorting, but maybe you become frustrated because you can't find homes for all the items, and your motivation starts to wane.

Another issue that can interfere with motivation is ambivalence. Ambivalence is the experience of having two contradictory thoughts at once. Think of a seesaw. On one side are all of the reasons you want to change, and on the other side are all the reasons you might want to stay the same. For example, maybe you decide to hold on to travel articles. You have a few monthly subscriptions and you have the stacks of articles set aside in your living room. It's been years since you've traveled, but you hope to get out there and experience the world again. On the other hand, it's been a while since you've had the chance to sit down and read them. You find yourself getting frustrated that the collection of articles is taking up so much space. The thought of getting rid of them seems absurd. If you let go of these articles, you fear you will lose good information, but you also want to take your space back.

EXERCISE: INCREASING YOUR LEVEL OF READINESS

Let's take a moment to dig into your readiness to tackle the clutter to assess how motivated you are. In your journal, rate on a scale from 0 (not at all) to 10 (extremely), your responses to the following questions.

- How important is it to you to work on your clutter?
- How ready are you to work on your clutter?
- How confident do you feel about working on your clutter?

Did conflicting thoughts arise? Thoughts that are in contrast indicate a discrepancy. When you notice these discrepancies, you are gaining an awareness of how some of your thoughts and beliefs may be working against your personal goals and values. What's the difference between goals and values? Think of your values as the driving forces that guide your actions toward achieving your goals. Here are a couple of prompts to respond to in your journal that will help you start identifying your values:

> What is important to you when it comes to relationships, personal well-being, career, hobbies, animal companions (if applicable), and finances?

> Are your saving and acquiring behaviors consistent with or competing with your personal values?

When you notice discrepancies, you can see which thought or belief aligns more with your personal values. Now, answer the following questions in as much detail as you can to increase your level of readiness:

- What could increase the level of importance of working on your clutter?
- What could increase your readiness to work on your clutter?
- What could increase your confidence to work on your clutter?
- What barriers need to be addressed so that you can work on your clutter?

Strategies for Staying Motivated

Now that you have some idea of what blocks your motivation, you're in a better position to keep yourself motivated with the strategies in this section.

1. MAKE A DECLUTTERING PROS AND CONS LIST

On a fresh page in your journal, make two columns labeled *Pros* and *Cons*. In the pros column, list all the advantages of working on your clutter, and in the cons column, list all the disadvantages. Some advantages might include "being able to have guests over" or "having the space to dedicate a room to my sculpting." Think of as many advantages as you can. What might be some disadvantages? Here are two examples: "I might accidentally get rid of something I cannot replace" and "I spent a lot of money on these things and it would be a waste to get rid of them." Write whatever you feel would be a disadvantage.

On your pros list, be sure to think of *all* the benefits of decluttering. To get a complete picture of your pros, it can be helpful to look at the cons of the clutter itself, such as the following:

- **Safety concerns**—tripping hazards, difficulty walking around the home with ease, difficulty accessing necessary items, such as a fire extinguisher; difficulty accessing doors and windows quickly; and so on (pro: "My home will be safer")

- **Impediments to socializing**—embarrassment and fear of having people in your home; thinking about the clutter while engaging in other activities, which interferes with your ability to fully enjoy yourself and be present (pro: "I'll be more social")

- **Financial problems**—concerns over finances or debt due to acquisitions (pro: "I can start getting a handle on my finances")

- **Emotional discomfort**—overwhelming feelings of anxiety thinking about tackling the clutter (pro: "I won't need to feel anxious about tackling the clutter, because I got it under control")

The things you've written on your cons list can make you feel uncomfortable. Did you know that feelings of discomfort can be a good thing? Yes, I am adding a positive spin to the word *discomfort*. If there is an absence of discomfort, you might not be motivated to work toward changing a problem. Therefore, you have identified a problem with your behavior, and you want to work toward changing that behavior. You can use the discomfort to your advantage.

Going Further with Pros and Cons

You can make pros and cons for virtually anything! Try it for acquiring items and not acquiring items. (What are the advantages and disadvantages of each?) You can also do this exercise with the items you're sorting. As you pick up an item, "think aloud" about its pros and cons. Be sure to include whether or not the item is in alignment with your goals and values (pros) or if it is out of alignment with them (cons).

2. WORK THROUGH DISCOMFORT

It's natural to feel anxious or scared when planning to declutter your home. It's also normal during the process itself. Engaging in "change talk" gives you an opportunity to recognize your feelings of discomfort and ask yourself some questions to test out your beliefs.

1. When you are noticing perfectionism (e.g., "I'll never be able to do it all, so what's the point?"), ask yourself,

   - Why does it have to be all or nothing?

   - What's the harm in trying a little bit even if that means I will not finish it all?

   - How does not trying to tackle your clutter fit in with my values?

2. When you are noticing anxiety (e.g., "Sorting makes me anxious. I cannot do this!"), ask yourself,

   - What specifically is making me feel anxious?

   - What do I think will happen if I decide to sort?

   - What would be so bad about trying?

   - What is the worst that could happen?

   - What is the best that could happen?

3. RIDE THE WAVE

It's normal to want to avoid stress as a way of protecting ourselves. How does the belief that stress will be intolerable show up in cluttering scenarios? Imagine that while sorting, you find something that triggers an unpleasant memory and discomfort. Suddenly, your mind tells you, "This is too stressful! It's time to get out of here!" So, you leave and try to find a way to self-soothe, perhaps by visiting your favorite store. Suddenly you are further away from your goals, you've made a purchase, and you have nowhere to put it, which leads to guilt and shame, which leads to more discomfort, creating a vicious cycle.

"Riding the wave" refers to gradually being able to face those feelings of discomfort so that the possession is no longer in control of you. Your emotions can fluctuate, but you can ride them like a surfer on a wave. When you stop avoiding your emotions and let them ebb and flow like the ocean without having to change them, you can continue working on your stuff and allow your values and goals to trump those negative emotions and feelings of discomfort. You do not need to acquire to make a bad feeling go away. The bad feelings will recede just like the waves on the shore.

Keep in mind that you will need to build up to this point. Start with the "easy button" (see page 46), and as time goes on, you'll be able to build your tolerance. With practice, dedication, and consistency, your definition of what's easy to let go of will evolve, and you will be able to handle the more difficult things.

4. EXPOSURE HIERARCHY FOR SORTING

An exposure hierarchy for sorting is a list of item categories ranked according to how triggering they are for you. This list can help you ride the wave by initially focusing on your least triggering categories. You'll gradually advance to more triggering categories.

In your journal, create a list of your home's item categories and rank them from 1 (easy to get rid of) to 10 (hard to get rid of). Dealing with the low-ranked categories will help you build up your tolerance for decluttering. Here's a sample list:

Office supplies	1
Newspapers	2
Shoes	3
Hats	4
Paperwork	5
Clothing	7
Gifts	9
Photos	10

5. DOWNWARD ARROW TECHNIQUE

The downward arrow technique is designed to combat negative thoughts as they appear to keep them from stopping you in your tracks. This technique can help you identify faulty thinking as well as any core beliefs that contribute to your saving and acquiring behavior along with avoidance of letting go. Keep asking yourself, "What would be so bad about that?" and "What is the worst that could happen?" This technique can help you learn more about yourself and the reasons you feel the need to hold on to items.

Here's an example using travel articles.

Q: "What would be so bad about letting go of some of the articles?"
A: "Well, I need them all in order to compare which places I want to visit."

Q: "What would be so bad if I can't make the comparison?"
A: "I might miss out on the better destination."

Q: "What's the worst that could happen?"

A: "I could end up having a terrible time."

Q: "What would be so bad about that?"
A: "I will have wasted all that money."

Q: "What's the worst that could happen if I wasted money?"
A: "I'll feel stupid and wasteful."

The downward arrow technique reveals embedded beliefs you have about yourself. Going through this process will help you test the probability that something bad will actually happen to you while also examining if your fears and beliefs are reasonable and valid.

Real-Life Story

Sharon had been tackling her clutter for a few months. She noticed periods where she was making great strides as well as moments of stagnation. She exhibited all of the classic "waxing and waning" symptoms associated with being motivated to achieve any behavioral change. She told me she was preparing for her brother to visit, and he hadn't been to the house in years. He was coming in from out of state, and her eagerness to share her home with her beloved brother strongly pushed her forward to make significant progress in her home. Her identified goals of having cleared surfaces and a clutter-free dining room (among others) were based on her personal values. She valued the idea of embracing her brother's company and comfortably sharing her home with him. She expressed wanting to sit and play dominoes at her table and reminisce without embarrassment or shame. While preparing her home, she chose to share her goals with some of her closest girlfriends. She recounted how freeing it felt to share her struggles with clutter with the people she valued most. That freeing feeling was further motivation to cut through the clutter.

6. TALK IT OUT WITH SOMEONE

Some people find it helpful and motivational to talk through their feelings, experiences, and struggles with someone, like a friend or a peer (someone you know who is also struggling with clutter). Attending a support group or even a virtual group can help (see Resources, page 150). In the support groups I facilitate, members have referred to each other as "clutter buddies." They contact each other outside of group to talk out issues rather than avoid the work. Talking with a friend who does not have this problem can be a scary thought. However, it can be part of cutting through the shame. True friends are people who support and love us. If you disclose in confidence that you are working on decluttering your home, how might it help you stop carrying that secret around?

7. CREATE AN INSPIRATION BOARD

To keep yourself motivated by your goals, create an inspiration board. You can use a corkboard or poster board. Pin or glue to it anything that inspires you. Let your creativity show! Inspirational ideas include quotes, images (including images of how you want your space to look), sayings, personal notes, and affirmations. Consider using bright colors and display your inspiration board in a highly visible space. Each time you glance over at it, you can feel a burst of inspiration.

EXERCISE: GET UNSTUCK—
YOU CAN MAKE A CHANGE NOW

You do not need to wait until it's the "right time" to make a change. Think about how long you have been wanting to work on your clutter or how many past attempts you've made. There's no better time than the present! As you get started, your motivation will continue to emerge, and you'll notice yourself generating momentum for additional work. But remember, keep your values and goals in mind to help you set your sights on the larger picture of how your life can be transformed by living a more organized life. Consider the following questions and journal your responses. Your answers will be revealing. I encourage you to add them to your inspiration board.

Think of a time in your life when you were able to overcome a great obstacle. By overcoming the obstacle, you demonstrated strength, productivity, motivation, and movement—all to accomplish some particular goal. Identify what approach you took to overcome the obstacle.

- What was the obstacle?
- What steps did you take?
- Who were the people in your corner who helped support you during that period?
- What beliefs did you have about yourself that promoted your success?
- What other factors contributed to your ability to handle that situation (e.g., spirituality, support systems, children, pets, etc.)?

8. PAIR IT WITH PLEASURE

It is no surprise that working on your clutter might not be the highest item on your bucket list. I'm sure there are plenty of other ways you would rather spend your time. Dreading the work can sap your motivation, so try pairing something pleasurable with your sorting. You can have a cup of your favorite tea before your sorting session and slip into your favorite comfy clothing. Perhaps you'll listen to your favorite music while sorting if it isn't too distracting and you can still think aloud while it's on. You can also try diffusing some uplifting scents into the air while you're doing the work.

9. CREATE A TIMED CHALLENGE

Challenging yourself to achieve a goal is a great motivational tool. Select a small target area and pick a goal. Maybe you will challenge yourself to sort the items on a tray table into their respective containers (keep, discard, and donate) in under 10 minutes. These short timed challenges in small target areas will help you practice your skills and strengthen your sorting muscle. While sorting, remember to pay attention to your emotions, thoughts, and actions, and think aloud.

10. TAKE TIME-OUTS

When the timer goes off after a 30-minute sorting session, give yourself a break, especially if you are planning to sort again. Spend some time doing something you find pleasurable, such as watching a TV show, scrolling through social media, taking a catnap or a walk, or another activity. Use this time as an opportunity to hit the "refresh" button so you can return to sorting with a renewed perspective. Taking breaks helps decrease the risk of mental and/or physical exhaustion. You are doing hard work, and you need to take care of you first!

11. CELEBRATE YOUR SUCCESS

No matter how small you perceive your achievement to be, you are taking steps forward in your process to declutter! Always take a few minutes to acknowledge your successes to yourself to keep your motivation level up. At the end of each week, state aloud all the tasks you accomplished that week. For example, you might say, "I donated a box of games to the local Y," "I found homes for all my kitchen utensils," or "I cleared the clutter off my couch." Maybe it's "I read this book!" If you're having trouble here, look at your SMART goals (see page 43), and view the before-and-after photos of areas you have already tackled. You might be surprised by how much you accomplished in a week's time.

12. PRACTICE THE GOLDEN RULE ON YOURSELF

You're probably familiar with the principle of doing to others as you would have them to you. By the same token, show yourself the same compassion and encouragement you would show others who are taking steps to overcome an issue. Think of what you would say to someone in a support group. In the groups I facilitate, I witness others being compassionate and encouraging with other members all the time but not giving themselves this same courtesy. For example, a group member may share discouraging words about themselves but jump in to support a member who says something similar. Be your own cheerleader on this journey. You may find your emotions take control and have you thinking, *I will never be able to get a handle on this clutter! What's the point in trying?* It's time to flip the script and encourage yourself with positive language: *I will get a handle on my clutter! I will be able to control it. I've been working on my clutter for a while now, but now I have new clarity because I have new strategies. I will translate the same strengths I demonstrated in overcoming my prior obstacles and use those strengths to overcome my clutter.* Being your own cheerleader can be just the motivational boost you need.

Conclusion

Hopefully, you've identified several ways to keep yourself motivated when your interest in sorting starts to wane, which it will from time to time. Just remember these helpful techniques and strategies and align yourself with your goals and values to keep yourself motivated to do what you've set out to do. As you proceed with this journey, consistently applying what you've learned can help you develop new habits that will bring you closer to your goals.

Self-Care Tip

Exercising your sorting muscle can be exhausting. If you are feeling physically depleted, spend time replenishing your physical needs. Stay hydrated by drinking plenty of water and other nonsugary drinks and keep yourself nourished by eating foods rich in nutrients. You cannot do this work if you are running on empty. So remember to keep yourself fueled.

CHAPTER FIVE

Transform the Way You Acquire Things

We live in a society where it's not uncommon to feel an impulse to make a purchase because there are advertisements all around us, drawing us in. The acquisition of things—whether it's a purchase we make for ourselves or a gift for someone else, whether it's new or used—plays a part in clutter. In this chapter, you'll take a look at your acquiring habits and learn ways to transform how you think about actively and passively acquiring items. You'll learn to think through acquisitions and discover techniques to resist urges.

What Attracts Us and Why

We will get to the strategies you can use to tackle acquisition, but first let's spend a few moments exploring the categories of items to which you find yourself most attracted. We all have our personal preferences for buying and acquiring things. One person may love to buy clothing; another, books and magazines; and yet another, multipurpose kitchen gadgets. Those items aren't necessarily the only things we buy. Our purchases and acquisitions might fall into several different categories. But it's good to be aware of what we are bringing into our homes and why. Let's take a look.

EXERCISE: WHAT DO YOU ACQUIRE MOST?

In your journal, list the five types of items you acquire the most with a few preliminary notes about why you like those items. Here's an example of what this list might look like:

1. **Clothing:** I like colorful and cozy sweaters and comfy pajamas.

2. **Gifts:** I can't leave a store without getting something for the children in my life.

3. **Secondhand furniture:** I have an eye for great pieces of furniture. I am not even looking to get something new, and then suddenly, I see a dresser on the side of the road with a "free" sign in front of it. How could someone get rid of something so beautiful?

4. **Art supplies:** I love the idea of creating beautiful things.

5. **Decorations and knickknacks:** Some things are just too pretty not to have.

Now, let's explore the thoughts that prompt your acquisition. Write down five thoughts that typically come up as you are encountering a new acquisition, such as the examples that follow.

1. I had a stressful week and buying this new sweater makes me feel better.

2. I have a couple of other things at home to give to kids, but I know this toy will really make one of them happy!

3. Not sure where I'm going to put this dresser, but I'll make room for it. It really is so beautiful. I need to stain it, but once I do, it will look as good as new.

4. I haven't used the paint set and canvas I already have, but they're for oil paints. Painting with acrylics on paper will be easier because it dries more quickly.

5. I know I haven't found a place for that figurine I bought recently, but this one will go perfect next to it.

Now, think about any emotions you experience before you make a purchase. Make a mental note of all the emotions you've experienced whether or not you resonate with the accompanying statements.

- Anxious: I've been so anxious lately and every time I get something new, I feel so much better.
- Sad: I got in an argument with my son about my clutter. He said I'm hopeless. Buying a couple new books always does the trick when I'm feeling down.
- Stressed: This week at work has been crazy! Retail therapy is the best.
- Irritable: My landlord is always butting in about my place and really needs to mind his own business.
- Guilt: I know I shouldn't go shopping because I already have so much at home.
- Happy: I just want to treat myself. I'm always doing for others, and I need to put me first.

Now, think about where the new purchase or newfound possessions go once you get back home. Which scenario resonates with you?

- They remain in the car.
- They remain in their bags by the front door.
- The tags and packaging are left on the purchases.
- You tend to forget about them afterward.
- You purchased a duplicate item because you forgot what you recently acquired.

You've answered quite a few questions here. Take a moment to reflect and look over your responses. This is an awareness-building exercise. Getting to know your acquiring habits is the first step to building strategies to overcome them.

Strategies to Stop Acquiring

Common reasons acquiring is problematic for many people is that they purchase items they do not have space for, experience debt, and even unintentionally purchase duplicate items. The strategies here offer you ways to change your acquisition habits to further your goal of a more organized lifestyle.

1. IDENTIFY ALTERNATIVE PLEASURABLE ACTIVITIES

People often assume they must abstain from their prior unhealthy behavior to develop new healthy behaviors. For instance, clients have told me that they will "just stop shopping and acquiring," but they end up reverting to their old behaviors when temptations arise. Avoiding your high-trigger locations or stopping this behavior abruptly and completely is not a sustainable long-term solution. A sustainable method is to change your reaction to factors that trigger you to acquire. You need to get to a place where you can walk into your high-trigger location and feel in control, which takes practice and exposure.

A good first step is to cut down on the behavior by engaging in alternative pleasurable activities. Let's say you go to garage sales on

Saturday mornings for fun and to find good deals. Or, on Friday evenings, you browse the Internet for things you might need. Instead, switch up your routine and schedule something you can do for enjoyment that doesn't involve acquiring anything aside from life experience.

In your journal, make a list of all the pleasurable activities you can do in place of your routine purchasing and acquiring habits. Get creative, and remember, it's okay to treat yourself to alternative sources of fun. Here are a few ideas:

- Go for a leisurely walk in nature.

- See a movie.

- Read a book in your collection you've been wanting to read.

- Get together with friends for a meal.

- Take an exercise class suited to your level of activity.

- Do yoga.

- Use your current craft supplies to create something new.

EXERCISE: IDENTIFY YOUR HIGH-TRIGGER LOCATIONS

The concept of retail therapy developed for a reason. Acquisition often serves a self-soothing purpose. Sometimes, people buy things when they are feeling sad and want a pick-me-up. Others buy items when they are happy and feel it's a nice way to reward themselves and keep themselves feeling good. Many people make impulse purchases after a long and stressful week, and some can't pass by the clearance rack without stocking up on items they might need down the road to ease their anxiety about the future. In all these cases, the items tend to provide some level of relief. Where these items are most often found and purchased depends on individual preferences.

Take a moment to think about some of your high-trigger locations. It feels impossible to pass by them, and you find yourself compelled to acquire something there, which makes your problems seem to disappear.

What are your high-trigger locations and why are they important to you? In your journal, name the locations and jot down what they mean to you. Now, make a list of items you normally acquire there. Again, this exercise is intended to build awareness. (If you make many of your purchases online, see strategy 9, Limit Online Shopping Triggers, page 81.)

2. PRACTICE PURCHASING ONLY CONSUMABLES

Because you need to bring things into your home to meet your daily needs, you obviously can't avoid acquiring indefinitely. Food, toothpaste, soap, shampoo, and paper goods, like toilet paper and paper towels, fall into the category of consumables. However, grocery stores and superstores where these items are found can be high-trigger locations for many people.

Take an inventory of what you already have in the way of consumables. Try not to spend too much time on this inventory. It's okay to guestimate. Look in your pantry. About how many canned and packaged goods do you have? Look in your refrigerator and freezer and check what you have. Also check on the quantity of your paper goods. This inventory will help you determine what you actually need to purchase to restock your supply (see the next strategy, Rule Creation, page 77). At the store, you may be tempted to buy things you don't need because they are on sale, but sales are just a way to get people to make additional purchases. Avoiding sales on things you don't need saves you money in the long run and helps you avoid wasting products in the future.

So, before shopping for food and other necessary items, with your inventory in mind, make a list of what you need and how much you can reasonably use before your next shopping trip. Write down a specific quantity for each item. Be sure to take into serious consideration whether you already have enough of that item on hand. If so, remove it from your list.

When you go to buy these items, it is imperative to stick to the list and practice purchasing only the consumables you listed in the quantity you can reasonably use. If a discounted item is not on your list, it means you didn't identify it as a need. For example, if you listed one package of toilet paper, buy only one package even if it is on sale. If you didn't list shampoo because you already have enough, it doesn't matter if it's discounted. Being mindful of what and how much you are purchasing helps you develop your nonacquiring muscle.

3. RULE CREATION

When you take your inventory, figure out how much of an item you need in each category. I recommend a concept I call "rule creation." With this strategy, you create your own rules about the quantity of an item to have on hand that makes sense to you and your life and aligns with your values and goals of tackling clutter and reducing acquisition. For example, maybe it makes sense to have six cans of tuna at any given time. If six cans of tuna are sufficient to keep your supply stocked, anything over six is too much and anything under six is not enough. Let's say you have four cans of tuna in your pantry. The rule you have created tells you that you need to purchase two more cans of tuna to replenish your supply. Rule creation is a way to keep track of your inventory, generate a shopping list, stick with your list, and reduce the urge to buy more than you need.

4. KEEP WRITTEN TRACK OF WHAT YOU BRING HOME

You've been practicing sticking to your grocery list and purchasing only consumables that you can reasonably use until your next shopping trip. Great! Now, think about what else you are bringing into your home. Anything that's not a consumable falls into this other category. It is easy to fall into the trap of just collecting things without giving it much thought or thinking about what really prompted the acquisition.

A way to become more mindful of what enters your home is to keep track of all your new acquisitions in your journal. You might think that simply keeping your receipts will do the trick, but it won't. Writing down your acquisitions will increase your awareness of your habits and highlight what you need to modify.

Keep your journal in a handy place. When something enters your home that wasn't there before, whether it's delivered to you or you go out and acquire it, immediately write it down in your journal along with the quantity. Ask yourself, "What was the rationale behind this new acquisition?" Think about whether or not your emotions influenced your decision-making process. Journal about it to become more aware.

5. WHAT ARE YOU GOING TO DO WITH RECEIPTS?

You may feel the need to hold on to your receipts for various reasons. Maybe you plan to compare them to your statements or enter them into a program to create a spreadsheet for budgeting purposes. Maybe you hold on to them in case the item breaks and you need to return it. These plans sound responsible, but when it comes to cluttering problems, such projects often get overlooked and items are seldom returned.

Ask yourself what you are *really* going to do with those receipts. If it is important to keep them, why? What is your plan for keeping them and when will you work on them? Compare this plan to any efforts you've already tried. For example, if at one point you were on top of updating your spreadsheet, how long did that last and what changed? Why wasn't that strategy successful for you? What makes you feel like you would be more successful this time? How long would it take you to keep up, and would you like to spend your time and energy that way?

Once you have gone through these questions, and you feel comfortable letting your receipts go, you can either shred or discard them. If you want to keep pertinent receipts, take time at the end of your sorting session to process them accordingly.

6. THINK IT THROUGH

No matter how you may try to stick to only consumables, triggers abound. You will likely encounter something that you feel like taking home with you. Simply telling yourself "I don't need it" is not enough. If you come across something you like and want to acquire, take the following steps:

1. Verbally describe the item.

2. Describe what you like about the item. Perhaps you like its utility, shape, and aesthetic qualities. Maybe you think it would make a great gift or a tasty treat.

3. Describe the qualities you do not like about the item. Perhaps that tasty treat would make your blood sugar spike, or you already have six cans of tuna and don't need any more.

Now ask yourself these questions:

- Do I have enough space for the item?

- Where do I envision putting the item?

- Will I use the item in the next one to two weeks?

- Do I have something like it already?

- If it is a gift, do I have a specific plan for gifting the item and by when?

- How would this acquisition help my goal of tackling my clutter?

- How would this acquisition hinder my goal of tackling my clutter?

- How would acquiring this item align with my values?

- In what way would this acquisition not align with my values?

7. PRACTICE WALKING AWAY

To get your new nonacquiring habits to stick, you'll need to start increasing your tolerance of uncomfortable feelings and unhelpful thoughts. When you come across an item you think you would like, practice walking away from the item, and leave the store if you have to. As you walk away, take note of the following:

- How does leaving the item make you feel? Perhaps you feel anxious, sad, angry, or disappointed. Maybe you feel something else. Just notice your predominate feeling(s).

- Rate each feeling on a scale from 0 to 10 (with 10 being intolerable and 0 being you notice minimal to nonexistent discomfort).

- Tune in to your thoughts. What are you thinking? Maybe you are thinking something like, *I'm afraid I am going to miss out on something I could really use.*

- What are your thoughts and feelings revealing to you about yourself?

Assuming you didn't go back and purchase the item, reevaluate how you feel about leaving that item behind five hours later. How about the next day? How about next week? You might notice that the feelings of discomfort and unhelpful thoughts lessen with time. This knowledge can help you the next time you are faced with something you feel the urge to acquire.

8. ONE IN, ONE OUT

An ongoing strategy you can use regarding any newly acquired item is to let something go in its place. If you decide to make a purchase of, let's say, a new vase, but you already have two or more vases, think about which vase you will let go of. When you bring home an item, ensure that something from that same category leaves your home, as either a discard or donation. This strategy can help with your clutter and acquisition reduction efforts. You can go a step further, too, and eliminate two items for every one new item you bring in, as one of my clients did. She bought a brand-new pair of yoga pants and donated one pair and discarded a pair that was irreparably torn.

9. LIMIT ONLINE SHOPPING TRIGGERS

Not all types of purchases are conducted in person. Maybe your high-trigger location is accessible to you from the comfort of your own home behind your computer, tablet, or phone. Let's face it: We live in the age of highly accessible products right at our fingertips; they're just a click away and can be delivered in two days' time.

All the strategies you're learning here also refer to online purchases. For example, if you enjoy spending time on electronic gadgets, try watching videos or playing a game, as you learned in strategy 1 Identify Alternative Pleasurable Activities (page 74). Or, if you are on your favorite shopping site and find an item you want, practice "walking away" from it for a day, as you learned in strategy 7, remembering to monitor changes in how you feel and what you're thinking as the day progresses and the following day.

10. CANCEL SUBSCRIPTIONS

Paper clutter often includes stacks of magazines, newspapers, articles, and other monthly or quarterly subscriptions. Acquiring these items through the mail is incredibly easy, and they can pile up quickly! If this problem applies to you, consider the written material that's being delivered to your home:

- How many subscriptions do you have?

- How many of them do you read?

- Do you find yourself saying, "I'll read that when I have the time," and then find yourself not revisiting that particular publication again?

- Have you noticed a pattern of telling yourself you'll get to it and then find yourself *not* getting to it?

If you answered yes to the last two questions, it's time to consider unsubscribing. If you're afraid you'll miss something, be mindful of online material that you can read on the topics you are interested in. When you unsubscribe, you'll immediately reduce how much stuff enters your home.

11. WHAT'S IN YOUR WALLET?

In your wallet and/or purse, you may have coupons, punch cards, gift cards, and other similar items that can prompt further acquisition. As you are working on reducing your tendency to acquire, challenge yourself to clear out these items to reduce the temptation to purchase more stuff. Ask yourself if the items these materials represent fit in with your goals and values. Question whether you really plan to use them, and if so, why. Maybe the coupons are advertising something you don't need or want to purchase. Perhaps the punch cards and gift cards are for a location you don't often visit. Because gift cards represent money, you'll want to hold on to them or give them to a friend or family member to use. Revisit the Think It Through strategy (page 79) for any potential purchases.

12. RETHINK YOUR CLIPPED COUPONS

Coupons represent things we want to purchase for a "better deal." They come in the mail and via e-mail, and they get handed to us as we walk into a store. They prompt us to use them to "save money." It's not uncommon to feel exhilarated because you bought something "at a bargain," but did you really need it? When it comes to coupons, ask yourself the following:

- Is the coupon valid? Discard coupons that have expired.

- Is the coupon usable at a place you visit regularly? You might keep a coupon because it seems like a great bargain, but if it's not useful at a location you visit regularly, it's not worth holding on to.

- Is the coupon advertising something you actually need? It's always great to get a bargain, but if you don't have an immediate use for it, you don't need the coupon.

- If you were to purchase the item advertised on the coupon, would it align with your values and goals? Do you have space for it when you get home? Will you regret making the purchase? Again, apply the Think It Through strategy (page 79).

13. THINK THROUGH BRINGING HOME A NEW ANIMAL

Struggles with acquisitions are not unique to inanimate objects. Some people experience an urge to acquire animals, especially when certain factors are at play, like finding a stray that looks like it really needs a home, visiting a local animal shelter, coming across a breeder's advertisement, and even walking by a pet store. Whether or not you have any animals already, think it through as you would any other acquisition:

- Ask yourself if getting a new pet will fit into your life right now. Think about how the new animal will feel in your space.

- Think through where in your home you would put all the animal-related belongings (such as a cage or tank, crate, litterbox, pet food, pet supplies, etc.).

- Will it be easy for you to take care of the animal if your home is cluttered? Think about how much more comfortable an animal would be in an uncluttered space. (Perhaps the idea of sharing your home with an animal can be a motivating factor for uncluttering!)

- Do you have the funds for all the things the animal would need, including vet bills and vaccinations?

- Do you have sufficient time to provide this new animal with all the attention it will require?

These are all important questions to consider when thinking about bringing home a new pet. When it comes to strays, reach out to your local animal welfare resource for assistance. Until you've more fully developed your nonacquiring muscle and you are absolutely sure you are ready to bring an animal into your life, avoid visiting shelters, pet shops, and breeders' websites.

14. EXPOSURE HIERARCHY FOR ACQUISITION

An exposure hierarchy for acquisition is a list of your high-trigger locations along with a rating of how triggering they are for you. Earlier in this chapter, you identified your high-trigger locations, and now it's time to rate them. In your journal, rate each location on a scale from 1 to 10 (with 1 being easiest to resist and 10 being hardest). You'll use these ratings in the next strategy. Here's an example to get you started:

High-Trigger Locations

Department store	10
Dollar store	3
Garage/yard sales	7
Grocery store	6
Hardware store	5
Online shopping	2
Thrift/consignment shops	4

15. REPLACE AVOIDANCE WITH GRADUAL EXPOSURE

You can't completely avoid high-trigger locations or stop acquiring things you need to live your life, so what can you do? Changing how you view and think about products can bring about a desired change in how you respond to them. You can begin this process by gradually exposing yourself to certain locations and practicing some typical alternative responses to making a purchase. Select a location you rated around a 5 or 6 in the previous strategy. Complete the following steps to help you gradually gain exposure and build your tolerance level.

1. Schedule a date and time to drive by the moderately difficult location. Do not pull into the parking lot or go into the store. Simply pass the location. Monitor how you felt by rating your feeling on a scale from 0 (no difficulty) to 10 (almost intolerable). When you get home, note your responses in your journal.

2. The following week, go to the same location and go into the parking lot. If you are in your car, park and sit there for five minutes. If you are walking, stand a distance away from the store for five minutes. (You can extend this period to 10 minutes if you feel able.) When you get home, again rate your feeling in your journal.

3. The following week, go to the same location and walk into the store. Briefly scan the location and then leave. Do not linger or walk around the store. Again, rate your feeling in your journal.

4. The following week, go on a "nonacquiring shopping trip." This exposure step is the last and most difficult. Go to the same location. Walk around the store and practice not purchasing anything. Monitor what you are feeling and thinking, what you are and aren't attracted to, and whether you feel an urge to acquire something. It helps to bring a notepad or your journal with you so you can write down your responses. As you rate how you feel while in the store, notice if the rating intensifies or lessens as you move to other areas. Practice picking up items and notice what you are thinking as you touch each item.

If you've taken all four steps and didn't buy anything, congratulations! If not, just continue to practice. After you've exposed yourself to a moderately difficult location, you can repeat the steps for more difficult or easier locations. This strategy helps you be present with what happens when you feel an urge and practice overcoming those urges.

EXERCISE: EXPLORE THE SHORT- AND LONG-TERM CONSEQUENCES OF ACQUIRING

This exercise helps you explore short-term and long-term consequences of the decisions you make around the acquisitions you bring home. You'll begin making connections by identifying your "hot spot" (or trigger), noting the action you took, and exploring the potential consequences of that action. In your journal, create a table like the example here. For each new acquisition, fill in a new row. This strategy will help you start to identify triggering moments, the action you took, and what you see as both the short-term and long-term consequence of your action. Again, this is an exercise in awareness.

TRIGGER	BEHAVIOR	SHORT-TERM CONSEQUENCE	LONG-TERM CONSEQUENCE
Drove by the thrift shop on my way home from a stressful visit with a family member.	Decided to stop in so I could use the 20% off coupon I got at my last visit.	I purchased a few items I didn't really need.	Added to my debt and took myself further away from declutter goals.

Conclusion

In this chapter, you learned how to look at your acquisition habits and pinpointed the locations where you acquire most frequently. You have many questions to consider when thinking about new acquisitions and techniques to avoid purchasing what you don't need. I hope you are ready to start exercising your nonacquiring muscle! Limiting the items you bring into your home will go a long way in helping you reduce your clutter and organize what you already have.

Self-Care Tip

Spend some time walking around a museum but plan
ahead to skip the gift shop (use the strategies in this
chapter if you need to). The idea is to take a self-care
break and simply be present to all the visuals, enjoying
the experience of looking at the beautiful creations and
displays. Notice how you can find pleasure in this activity without making a purchase. The life experience you
acquire will be nourishing rather than distressing.

CHAPTER SIX

Build Your Support Team

We all need a team of supportive people in our corner when we actively tackle an issue we want to change. The same applies for reducing clutter and limiting what you bring into your home. A support team consists of people you can rely on to talk through your challenges, frustrations, and successes. Talking with others also reduces the stigma associated with cluttering by helping you cut through the shame. Your support team can help you stay motivated to reach your goals. Plus, you can test out the strategies you've been learning with other people, as well!

What Has Your Experience Been Like?

I know that feelings of shame and embarrassment often accompany a cluttering problem, but opening up to others about your struggles helps lift that heavy emotional burden you've been carrying around. People you elect to disclose this information to can be part of your emotional and/or physical support system. However, you must take a strategic, methodical approach to developing your supporters. Maybe you've had experiences with family members or others who have hindered your progress because working with them was primarily a negative experience. Perhaps they tried to take charge, and you no longer felt like you were in control. Or perhaps they were really helpful, but you weren't in the right place to appreciate their help. Before we get started on the strategies in this chapter, let's look at where you've been.

EXERCISE: REFLECT ON PAST EXPERIENCES WITH OTHERS

Think about the time(s) you allowed other people to help you with your clutter in the recent or distant past. Write your responses to the following questions in your journal:

- Who tried to help you?
- Why did you select that person to work with you?
- How and why did you ask that person?
- How long did that person help you (hours, days, weeks, months)?
- What made this experience helpful to you?
- What wasn't helpful about this experience, and why?
- Think about the ways this person's help could have been improved.
- Would you ask this person to help you again? Why or why not?

Your answers to these questions will set the tone for the strategies in this chapter. Maybe your experience was positive or negative. We'll focus on ways to enhance the process of working with other people.

Building Your Team

The following strategies can help you find the support you need and prepare you to communicate to others how they can assist you in reaching your goals.

1. SEEK PROFESSIONAL HELP

Tackling clutter is much more than just dealing with your stuff. There's a lot of internal work that needs to occur, such as paying attention to your thoughts, emotions, and behaviors and actions. This book provides strategies to help with both internal and external processes, but it can also be helpful to find a professional to help you continue to combat distressing thoughts, feelings of anxiety, a sense of being overwhelmed, and lack of motivation. Here are some guidelines:

- Search for a mental health professional, such as a psychologist, psychiatrist, social worker, or mental health counselor, who has experience working with clients who have hoarding or cluttering issues.

- If you cannot find a mental health professional who has experience in this area, find one who is trained in CBT. This kind of therapy is the preferred treatment modality for working with clutter because it focuses on behavior modification, understanding thoughts and emotions that motivate the behavior, and the implementation of skills and strategies (learning to sort and discard) to help sustain your new behavioral efforts. You can conduct an online search for therapists in your area. (See the Resources section, page 150.)

Questions for a Potential Professional Organizer or Cleanup Support Team Member

When you are interviewing a professional organizer and/or cleanup support specialist, consider their answers to the following to make an informed decision:

1. How long have you been organizing/working as a cleanup specialist?

2. Do you have experience working with people who clutter?

3. How many cases have you worked pertaining to clutter?

4. What were the results of those working relationships? Can you provide references who I can contact?

5. How long do you typically remain involved with these cases?

6. How do you define success in such cases?

7. Do you have professional training or hold certifications in organizing, hoarding remediation, or related areas?

8. Have you attended trainings/conferences on hoarding and cluttering? If so, how many? What stood out to you from attending those trainings?

9. Will I work directly with you, or will you assign another employee to the case? If so, how do you determine who would make the best decluttering partner in working with me?

10. What is a typical working session like? How long will we work for? Over how many sessions? With how many people? How long does an average case take?

11. How much do you charge for your services? What do these fees entail?

12. Will you give me a written contract?

13. What is your cancellation policy?

14. I have worked with other professionals/and or tried to get organized before. Can you tell me how your service will be different?

15. What is your process if you notice a client getting overwhelmed during an appointment?

- Counselors are not the only ones who can help with this issue. You can also try professional organizers (see the Resources section, page 150) and even life coaches. Professional organizers and life coaches can assist by helping you stay motivated, explore barriers to your motivation, and create organizational standards that make sense for your needs.

- Other resources include physical support in the form of cleanup companies. However, be aware of overly aggressive workers who want to take charge. You need support and encouragement throughout this process, not someone who wants to do the work for you. If you rely on others to clear your clutter, you run the risk of not gaining insight into your issue or learning from doing the work yourself. Don't enlist the help of someone who thinks the solution is to do a full cleanup. Connect with companies that can help with sorting and cleaning, if needed. Develop a contract that outlines the work and describes boundaries.

2. CONNECT WITH A COMMUNITY OF LOCAL PEERS

You are not alone, and I can't emphasize this fact enough. There are millions of people who self-identify as having a hoarding or clutter problem and are looking to connect with their peers. Attending a group can be a great start. It can normalize your experiences, which helps reduce the associated shame and embarrassment. The more you hear other people identifying clutter as an issue they want to work on, the more you'll notice a decrease in your negative thoughts.

As mentioned earlier, negative thoughts are highly prevalent in people with this challenge. By surrounding yourself with peers, you'll notice this negative self-dialogue beginning to shift. Plus, most support groups follow some group protocol, agenda, or format that provides you with an opportunity to learn more about why you clutter and test out new ways to tackle the clutter. Last, peers often learn from each other and find ways to test out strategies together, so this process can even help you become more social. Here are a few ways to find in-person support groups:

- Conduct a general search online for local hoarding task forces. There is a likelihood that the task force (even if farther away) can help you locate a nearby support group.

- Connect with your local senior center, where clutter-reduction support groups are often held.

- Some support groups are facilitated by mental health professionals. Inquire by calling therapists in your area.

See the Resources section (page 150) for further suggestions.

3. LOCATE AN ONLINE COMMUNITY

In-person peer support groups are not the only way to connect with others. There are many online resources and virtual communities you can join to connect with other people where you can receive and share suggestions for reducing clutter and cheer each other on. Some online groups are open groups, meaning anyone can join, but other groups are closed and you need to be accepted by an administrator to become a member (which often applies to in-person groups, as well). I recommend joining an online community to supplement an in-person group, but if you are unable to attend one, an online community can be a great source of support. (See the Resources section, page 150.)

4. FIND A CLUTTER BUDDY

Once you join an in-person group or online community (or both), you may find yourself really connecting with the other members. Group members often feel a heightened sense of wanting to share their pitfalls and successes and how they are feeling. After facilitating many groups over the years, I noticed that members wanted to stay connected even outside of group meetings. Collectively, we came up with the term "clutter buddy." (Notice that we put a positive spin on the term *clutter*.)

A clutter buddy is someone you can check in with outside of meetings, such as a social call or a time to engage in wellness and alternative pleasurable activities together. You can reach out to your clutter buddy when you are having a tough time working on your goals, if your thoughts or emotions take a downturn, or even when feeling triggered to go out acquiring. A clutter buddy can also come to your home to help you sort by utilizing the strategies in this book and applying techniques you learned in your group.

5. CREATE A SUPPORT GROUP

If you feel driven to attend an in-person support group but there aren't any in your area, create one! More and more groups are popping up this way. When considering starting a group, identify what you hope to accomplish and what you would like the group to look like. You can have an informal group of just a few people where you talk about your struggles and find inspiration to propel yourself and the other members forward. Here are a few ideas:

- Spread the word online. You may be surprised by how many members who live within traveling distance will be attracted to the idea of a local in-person group. If you are looking for an in-person group, chances are your peers are, too.

- Advertise in public places, like the library and senior centers.

- Locate a private space for your group where you can share openly, such as a room at a restaurant, library, recreation center, VFW post, senior center, housing/apartment community room, or house of worship. Many of these places are willing to host peer-led groups; all you need to do is ask around. When you find a suitable space, reserve it as a recurring appointment (weekly, bimonthly, or monthly, depending on the group's preferences).

- When you have a few members, they can help build the group by spreading the word.

- Share with members that you're new to forming a support group and ask what they would like to see with regard to the group structure and how can you collectively make this group beneficial for everyone.

Studies indicate that peer-led support groups can be just as powerful as clinician-facilitated support groups. With this approach, you are building a network of people you trust. There's no reason you have to tackle your clutter problem on your own in isolation.

6. SET BOUNDARIES WITH LOVED ONES

Everyone has different experiences when it comes to family and friends helping them reduce clutter. Some people choose to forgo their help entirely due to adverse past experiences, but others are willing to give it another try. One strategy to allow others to help is to set healthy boundaries by voicing what you really need assistance with and how the process can help you.

An extra set of hands can go a long way, but you need to outline what needs to be done. When enlisting the help of friends and family, set clear boundaries to keep everyone on the same page and protect your time together. Avoid assuming your loved ones know what's appropriate. Here are some guidelines:

- Generate an outline of tasks with which you need assistance. Set boundaries regarding these tasks.

- Clearly communicate that the decision of whether to keep an item or let it go is entirely up to you.

- Welcome suggestions for relocating items to other areas with similar possessions.

- Be open to ideas that can help you make a decision and explore them with the understanding that the ultimate decision is yours.

- Communicate your limits regarding time and effort, and request that the person helping you respect them. It's key not to push yourself. If you feel pushed beyond your tolerance level, the collaborative process can be hindered, which you want to avoid.

- Express that this process is hard for you and that you may feel embarrassed by needing and allowing the other person to help. This process requires empathy.

- Come up with a plan for the collaborative work. Agree on how long and how often to accept the help. Is this assistance a onetime opportunity or something you may agree to do daily, weekly, or monthly? Outline a clear time frame for the duration of the assistance per session, perhaps an hour or two or more.

7. IDENTIFY TARGET AREAS WITH YOUR HELPERS

Earlier, you learned strategies for choosing a target room and a target area within that room. When you are working with someone, clearly identify the area you want to focus on. Describe the help you need. Sticking to one area at a time is critical, so clearly outline exactly where you need the help and stick to that area together. The idea is to combine your efforts on that one target area. Maybe you will work on your closet and sort through some clothing. Perhaps you'll sort paperwork on the kitchen table and you need some assistance creating a filing system. Pick your helper's brain on what they think is reasonable to keep and what can be shredded.

8. DO NOT REWRITE THE SCRIPT

When working with other people, stick to the strategies you've been practicing. Reinventing the process can create an opportunity for the work to unravel. For example, continue using the sorting categories you've created: keep, donate, and discard. You can let the person helping you take a look at this book and point out the strategies you're currently practicing.

9. CREATE SMART GOALS FOR ASSISTANCE

When you've found someone you feel comfortable working with, create SMART goals (see page 43). Remember, SMART goals are specific, measurable, attainable, relevant, and time-bound. Arrive at these SMART goals together. Make specific agreements on how often to accept the help, what that help will involve, what to focus on during helping sessions, and how long that help will continue. Some clutter buddies like to create SMART goals to work on between helping visits, such as tasks or "homework" to commit to and accomplish prior to the helper's next visit. Remember to keep your goals manageable.

10. ESTABLISH A FOCAL POINT

Prior to sorting with your helper, discuss some ways you believe that person can help you stay on track if your attention is starting to fade. For instance, a client of mine once told me that she and her partner came up with a "focal point": He would hold his hands in a circle that symbolized the focal point in her garden, which she loved. If he noticed her getting sucked into an article and stopped responding to some of his questions, he would simply call out her name and make the gesture. This focal point helped her laugh it off, and they would continue their work for the designated amount of time. Think of the ways your partner can help you refocus, or describe how best to point out what they can do if they notice you are losing focus.

11. TAKE SCHEDULED BREAKS

When you are working with a helper, just as you would if you were working alone, take regularly scheduled breaks. Agree ahead of time how long you will work before taking a break and how long that break will be. Taking breaks can help you avoid burnout. A break can be as simple as having a cup of tea together or doing something separately for the allotted time.

12. REWARD YOURSELF AND YOUR HELPER

When making an agreement to work together on your clutter, also make an agreement to do something pleasurable afterward as a reward. Having something to look forward to can help you both stay motivated to complete your agreed-upon task for the day. Here are some ideas for rewarding activities:

- Have a meal or a cup of coffee together either at a restaurant or in your home.

- Go to or watch a movie you've both been wanting to see.

- Play a game, like cards or dominoes.

- Go for a stroll around the neighborhood or at the park.

When possible, do a fun activity in your home. Being able to enjoy your cleared space reminds you that your home is not just the setting for hard work but a place where you can reap the benefits of your labors.

EXERCISE: WHO DO YOU WANT ON YOUR TEAM?

In your journal, make a list of all the people you want on your team who you believe will be helpful to you in your journey. Think it through carefully. Your list can include people you already know and also people you hope to connect with (group members, therapists, or other professionals). Then make a plan to reach out and ask for help.

13. MONITOR YOUR EMOTIONS AND TOLERANCE LEVELS

While working with other people in your home, pay attention to how you are feeling, what you are thinking, and what your behaviors are revealing to you. Are your emotions improving, remaining the same, or worsening? This strategy helps you gauge these changes.

Prior to a helper coming to your home, take note of the following:

- Your feelings—for example, *This feels intrusive. I'm feeling a little scared.* Rate the feeling on a scale from 0 to 10—for example, *It feels like a 7 out of 10.*

- Your thoughts—for example, *What if this person changes their opinion of me because of my cluttered home? What if they no longer want to help me or, worse, no longer want to be my friend?*

- Your actions and what they are telling you about yourself—for example, *I noticed I'm trying to clean up so I feel more comfortable with this person coming over.*

While the helper is in your home, take note of the following:

- Your feelings—for example, *I'm feeling nervous.* Rate how you are feeling on a scale from 0 to 10.

- Your thoughts—for example, *I think they're secretly judging me*, or *This isn't as bad as I thought.*

- Your actions and what they are telling you about yourself. Are you actively working with the person? Are you openly communicating with them? Are you noticing yourself becoming more guarded and withdrawn?

When the helper has left, go through this process again. What are you feeling (rate it), what are you thinking, and what are your actions telling you about yourself? Your answers can be revealing. They may show you that you are anticipating something worse than what actually occurs, or they may suggest you need to have a conversation with your helper about how you are feeling and brainstorm ways to make this process more constructive for both of you.

Real-Life Story

My client Matthew was social and quite admired. However, the people he often associated with were not aware of his painfully hidden secret. He believed he would never be able to let his loved ones know about his hoarding issue. Over time, he started talking about wanting some support to help him make faster progress. He had spent months making great strides in his home and did a lot of work on not only reducing his clutter but also raising his mental awareness. One day he disclosed to me that he'd been contemplating asking two of his closest friends to help him sort through some of his clothing. He knew asking them would be difficult, but he felt it was important to have support while he made decisions to keep or let go of clothing that held such significance to him. We prepped for what it would be like having his friends support him in his home, as they hadn't seen it in its current state. Because these men had been close friends for a long time, he felt confident they would continue to love him regardless of what he was going through. Afterward, he told me how the visit went. He said they had fun with it, and he put on a "fashion show" wearing various outfits. They had several good laughs. He remarked that the experience was liberating and recounted how good it felt to shed clothing he no longer needed but also, and more important, how good it felt to shed the burden of feeling like he couldn't share all parts of himself with friends, including his silent struggle with clutter. Shortly after this excursion, Matthew related his experience to the members of his group. He said that although it was difficult for him to share this vulnerable side of himself with his friends, the process helped him cut through the shame.

Helpful Tips for Your Supporters

You've been reading this book to learn strategies to reduce your clutter and how best to enlist the help of others, but this part of the book is specifically for those whose help you are enlisting. Let them know you've been reading this book and working on the strategies. Although they are welcome to flip through this book and read the strategies, ask them to read this section specifically.

WHAT TO DO AND NOT DO WHEN HELPING

When you are helping someone with a clutter problem, it is important to keep some key concepts in mind to create confidence in the person you are trying to help. Follow these guidelines:

- Do not use harsh or judgmental language.
- Do not touch items without explicit permission from the person you are helping.
- Do not declutter behind their back.
- Do not make decisions for the person or try to persuade them to let something go.
- Do not equate the person with the clutter.
- Do not minimize any challenges they are facing.
- Model positive and adaptive behavior.
- Provide encouragement and emotional support.
- Have faith in their ability to make decisions and take action.
- Highlight their strengths and provide positive validation.
- Stay calm, even when it feels tough. Take breaks as needed.
- Follow through on tasks you volunteered for.

WHAT TO SAY WHEN PROVIDING SUPPORT

When working with someone who has a clutter problem, the language you use is very important. The words you choose can show that you empathize and that you want to help, not take charge of the situation. Maybe you've had conversations with this person in the past that did not go so smoothly. Flip the script by learning some positive communication. It make take a few attempts to rebuild trust and let them know you genuinely care and want to assist. For example, when speaking with your loved one about the clutter, begin with a positive statement, such as "I love you very much and I value our relationship."

Try to use the word *I* instead of *you*. When you say something like "You really shouldn't buy that," it can come across as harsh judgment. Instead, you can say something more like "I can see that you value that item and you would like to purchase it. I worry that bringing that item home will take you further from your goals of working on your home."

Express understanding and share responsibility. For example, you could say, "I understand that it is hard for you to accept my help. I know I haven't made things easy in the past, but I am trying to understand and help you the best way I can. I hope we can work on this together."

Conclusion

In this chapter you focused on ways to build your team to best support your efforts as you work toward tackling your clutter. You took the time to review what your ideal team would look like and what to do with their help once you have agreed to get started. Staying on track with your goals can be a team effort; there is no shame in asking for help and staying in control.

Self-Care Tip

You did a lot of hard work! Reward yourself by taking yourself out to a movie, a play, or the opera. This can give you a mental break to destress and unwind. One of the nicest things you can do for yourself is buy a ticket to a movie or show you've been wanting to see. Sit back, relax, and enjoy the show!

PART THREE

TACKLING THE CLUTTER AND CLEARING YOUR MIND

This part of the book discusses sorting and organizing your home with specific, room-by-room strategies. Although they appear in a certain order, you get to choose the target rooms and target areas you want to work on first. To help you maintain long-term success, this part concludes with suggestions to keep you in control of your possessions.

CHAPTER SEVEN

Let's Get Organized: Room-by-Room Strategies

In this chapter, you'll learn how to develop a more organized space, which includes the sorting strategies you've been learning, in a room-by-room fashion. Keep in mind that I've included common areas in a house, but your home may be set up differently. You can still use these guidelines by adapting the suggestions as needed. For example, if you don't have a dedicated office, you may still have a desk somewhere in your home that you use for your paperwork. In this way, the office section still applies.

Always remember that sorting precedes organization. Sorting prepares you to organize more efficiently and in a more meaningful way because you've let go of the things you felt comfortable releasing and the overabundance of stuff is diminished. Now you have set yourself up for successfully organizing your possessions and achieving your goals of leading a simpler lifestyle. When your home is organized, you'll be able to locate things when you want them and move around with more ease. You'll also be proud of your space. This chapter brings you several steps closer toward reclaiming your life!

11 Key Organizational Principles

While you are sorting and organizing your home, refer to this master list of key organizational principles as often as you need to:

1. **Sorting precedes organization:** As a rule, prior to organizing, you must set aside time to sort through your belongings and put them in their keep, discard, or donate container. The idea is to put your "keep" items where they belong (with like items) after your sorting session. However, if doing so is not possible right away, group the belongings you are keeping into their own categories—for example, clothing with clothing, kitchen gadgets with kitchen gadgets, and so on (see the strategy on page 42). Once you see what you have, you will likely identify things you can let go of because you already have enough or as much as you can find homes for.

2. **Put away now, not later:** Get in the habit of putting things away in their designated place. Doing so can help you minimize the chance of reaccumulating things in areas you have worked hard to declutter and maintain.

3. **Schedule time to sort and organize:** Set a schedule and stick to it to achieve your organizational goals. Mark your calendar as if setting an appointment with someone important, which in this case is you! At the end of the day, initial next to your appointment if you sorted and/or organized for the day, and jot down the amount of time you spent on it.

4. **Don't be hard on yourself:** If your thoughts become negative and you start giving yourself a hard time, it's time to take a break. Step away for a little while and then return to the work when you are in a calmer state. Treat yourself the way you would treat a friend: with kindness and compassion.

5. **Do a little bit each day:** Work for 30 minutes to one hour each day. Select a target area (for example, your bedroom closet) and see it through before you move on to the next area. Always start small to avoid getting overwhelmed. Continue using your SMART goals (see page 43) to help you develop reasonable and manageable organizational tasks.

6. **Measure progress with before-and-after photos:** Take photos before and after you organize. Having evidence that you are indeed working toward your organizational goals can keep you motivated to continue working.

7. **Use organizational bins as needed and label them:** Purchase clear, sturdy, stackable, airtight containers to protect the contents of what you are keeping, preferably after you have sorted your designated areas so you have a better sense of how many you need. They don't have to be expensive; bins like these are available in a variety of stores.

8. **Get others on board:** If other people live in your home, including children, get them to help by putting items away in their respective labeled bins or spaces. Make sure labels are clear and legible so that others can stay on task. Everyone in your home can work as a team to achieve organization.

9. **Allow yourself to let go:** Give yourself permission to let items go. Ask yourself the 10 decision-making questions on page 52 to help you get there.

10. **Live in the present:** Remind yourself to live in the here and now. The time to change is now. The time to organize is now. The time to be in control and reclaim your life is now.

11. **Prioritize safety and functionality:** Think safety first, always. When you are striving for clearer and more organized spaces, work toward a safer home.

Kitchen and Dining Room

REFRIGERATOR

An overstuffed refrigerator can interfere with proper air circulation and result in a less energy-efficient appliance, among other drawbacks, such as not being able to find what you need. Start by doing a thorough cleaning of your refrigerator. Dispose of all products that are beyond their expiration dates. Pay attention to what you are discarding. If a product is expired, maybe you don't consume it enough to purchase again. Not buying these products can help you minimize waste. Discard any condiments beyond their expiration date, as well, even if you do use condiments relatively frequently. They are easy to replace. Any items without clear expiration dates that you know have been around for a while can also be discarded.

Once you've discarded all the items you're not keeping, wipe down the shelves and organize your refrigerator. Here are a few guidelines:

- Store similar food items together.

- Place produce in the produce drawers at the bottom of the fridge and check often.

- Put leftovers in storage containers so they are easily identifiable, rather than leaving them in takeaway boxes.

- Store meat and seafood on the middle shelf (the coldest part of the refrigerator).

At the end of each week, discard older leftovers or spoiled items, and clean up any spills. To help ease you into disposing of old and expired food products, investigate compost collection in your area.

FREEZER

As you did with your refrigerator, go through the freezer the same way. Discard all questionable items. The presence of freezer burn can help you make your decision, as can expiration dates. Although frozen, if an item is past its date, consider if you plan to eat it and/or serve it to guests. If you hesitate, it's time to let it go. No longer having interest in consuming a certain food is an indication, too, that you may want to dispose of it. If you have ice trays or an ice container, throw out the ice and wash and dry the trays or container before refilling. Old ice can be a breeding ground for bacteria.

PANTRY

Many homes have a separate pantry closet or small room for storing boxed, bagged, jarred, and canned goods as well as paper goods. In smaller homes, one or more kitchen cabinets may serve this purpose. Whatever form your pantry takes, sort through the items you have on hand. Check expiration dates and discard any items past their date. If a product is not expired and still sealed, but it's not likely you or someone in your home will consume it, look into donating it to your local food bank.

Organize items with like items. For example, group all the cans together, all the boxes together, all the paper goods together, and so on. Then you can place similar items in the space you've set aside for them: pasta with pasta, rice with rice, and so on. Use clear containers to hold opened dried products (such as flour or sugar). If you use things like flour and sugar frequently, you can keep them on your kitchen counter in designated containers. Label the containers with the expiration dates on the package to eliminate confusion.

If you have the space, install a wall-mounted rack to hold your spices or get a revolving tray so that you can easily locate the spice you need.

Once you've organized what you have, create an inventory list, for example, 8 cans of beans, 2 jars of olives, 3 cake mixes, 4 boxes of cereal, and so on. Tape this list inside your pantry door and update it as you use an item. You can also use a small dry-erase board for easy upkeep. This inventory can help you generate your grocery list so that you refrain from buying what you don't need. Of course, if maintaining

First In, First Out (FIFO)

When I was younger, I worked in the restaurant industry for many years. I learned a valuable concept that I share with my clients today called FIFO (first in, first out). When you purchase a new food product, place it behind an identical food item you already have. This way, you will consume the older items first and limit potential waste. Use the FIFO concept for your pantry items, freezer, and refrigerator.

an inventory list proves to be too much, simply keep a grocery list and add items as you use them.

EXERCISE: 15-MINUTE PANTRY CLEAN-OUT

Take a photo of your pantry before you sort and organize, and then set your timer for 15 minutes. Shelf by shelf, separate items into "keep," "discard," and "donate" groups. Discard items that are expired or questionable. Donate sealed unwanted or excess products that are still within their expiration dates. Once you have your discard and donate piles, take a photo of them. Also, take another photo of your pantry. These photos are evidence of your progress. Reflect on the photo of what you are not keeping. You may not need to purchase those items again.

CABINETS AND DRAWERS

Sort through all your kitchen cabinets and drawers to condense their contents to only "keep" items. Target one cabinet or drawer at a time. Plan to discard any peeling, bent, or cracked items.

Pull out all your pots, pans, and casserole dishes and ask yourself if you've used them more than once. If not, perhaps you don't need that cookware and you can donate it if it's still in good condition. Do the same with your cooking utensils. Gather all spatulas, wooden spoons, and the like. Consider placing the ones you use regularly in a decorative holder that sits on your kitchen counter. This storage method frees up space in the drawers and prevents the utensils from clattering around when you open and close the drawers. It also makes it easier to grab them during your cooking and baking adventures.

Really think about those fancy all-purpose utensils and gadgets. If you've used them only once or not at all, they may be good items to include in your "donate" pile.

Tackle your plates, cups, and dishes with an eye toward damage. Anything that's cracked or chipped can be recycled or discarded. Gather plates and organize by category: serving dishes, saucers, dessert plates, dinner plates, and so on. Stack the plates from largest on the bottom to smallest on top to optimize your storage space. Gather all serving dishes and stack by size. Keep daily-use cups and mugs in easy-to-access areas. If you are worried about space to house your mugs, install hooks under your upper kitchen cabinets to hang them up. This way you can add decorative flair and also keep your mugs accessible and organized. Decorative cups and mugs can also be stored in a dining hutch or in other cabinets.

Once you've sorted all the items in your cabinets and drawers, it's time to organize: Create sections and keep similar items together. Stack pots, pans, and casserole dishes to generate more space in lower cabinets. Keep the lids near the pots and pans in an organized fashion. Measure the dimension of your drawers and purchase organizing inserts at your local home goods store to keep smaller items, like silverware, contained. Gather all your kitchen knives and place them in their knife block on your kitchen counter. If you don't have one, you can purchase a universal knife block to help keep all of your knives orderly.

Label each shelf where you can readily see the label as a reminder of what goes where. Labels might include "pots/pans" and "bakeware."

Set a daily maintenance goal to remove washed dishes from the dishwasher or counter and put them in their respective homes. This task may seem simple but is often overlooked. Putting dishes away daily can keep you on track in maintaining your organized home.

COUNTERTOPS

When working on your kitchen, I suggest tackling storage areas first (cabinets, drawers, and pantry). Organizing your storage areas will prompt you to put similar items on your countertops into their designated spaces.

Keeping your countertops cleared and organized will free up surfaces for meal preparation and also create a space that reflects your aesthetic preferences. However, you may want certain things on your countertops so they are accessible. Think about the tools you use regularly. These items may include paper towels in a holder, a knife block, a coffee maker, and a decorative holder for cooking utensils. For safety purposes, ensure that at least six inches on either side of your stove (depending on design) are always clear.

Kitchen counters can become a catchall for mail and other miscellaneous items. I address daily mail in the office section on page 132, but the same strategy applies to mail and other papers that accumulate in this common area.

STOVE TOP AND OVEN

To prevent a fire, keep your stove top clear of debris and clutter. If you have any items currently on your stove top, move them to a drawer or cabinet. If you have anything in your oven, remove it and place it in its new home. If you don't have a home for it because you have limited room in your kitchen and the item is not flammable, you may have no choice but to store it there. However, many ovens have a pull-out drawer at the bottom. Use this drawer to hold flat bakeware and pans if needed.

KITCHEN/DINING ROOM TABLE

Because tables are flat surfaces, they (like kitchen counters) can also become a catchall for paperwork, mail, and random items. Refer to page 132 for dealing with your daily mail and other paperwork. Reroute any other items to their proper locations to avoid accumulation on your table(s). Once you've cleared your table, set it and keep it that way to create a visually inviting look, which can help you also keep it clear.

HUTCH

If you have a hutch in your kitchen or dining room, it may fall into that catchall dilemma. Yes, a hutch serves as good storage, but try to be mindful of the way you would like to utilize that storage. Think of the things you absolutely need to have in your hutch and reroute the rest. Some examples of things to store in your hutch include decorative/seasonal china, serving dishes/platters, glasses, mugs, and various decorations.

Entry, Living Room, and Family Room

ENTRYWAY

An entryway needs to be kept clear for safety. If there are items blocking your entryway, reroute those items to elsewhere in your home. Ask yourself if there's an alternative spot for the item. If it's something you wish to keep but you don't have a dedicated space for it, place it in a clearly marked storage bin and put it in storage. Install decorative hooks near your entryway for your guests to hang their jackets on, and set up a bench near your entryway where they can take off their shoes on wet and snowy days. Place lined baskets underneath the bench to store shoes. You can also store a pair of your everyday shoes in the basket to keep them off the floor.

ENTRYWAY CLOSET

Sort through your coat closet, which is often near your entryway, and try on all jackets, sweaters, and coats. Donate items that no longer fit or are no longer relevant to you. Keep all your coats, hoodies, and so on in this closet rather than in your bedroom closet. If there's space, install hooks on the inside of the closet wall or door to hold scarves, hats, and paired gloves. A shelf can work for these items, as well. If you don't have a shelf in your coat closet, install one for additional storage. If there are other items in your entryway closet that fit categories you've created elsewhere, reroute them after sorting.

BOOKS, NEWSPAPERS, AND MAGAZINES

I do not want to downplay the usefulness, wonder, and knowledge that can be found in books. However, maybe you do not need all of them. Sort through your books and pay attention to general themes of the ones you enjoy the most. Maybe you love history or even a certain era of history. Then by all means, keep the books that speak to you. But look at some other subject areas and think if some of those books can benefit someone else. Donate accordingly. A book that has been sitting in your home unread could really be meaningful to another person.

Once you have sorted through your books, bookshelves are a great way to display these treasured items. Try not to get hung up on how to categorize the books—when in doubt, stick with general categories (history, art, cooking, philosophy, etc.). If such genres make sense for you, place labels on the shelves. Do not try to create more work for yourself. Get them up and organized on shelves.

Gather all the cookbooks, food magazines, and cooking articles. Sort through them to determine what is still relevant to you and question your likelihood of preparing each recipe. Recycle or discard all the others. Place all the keepers on your bookshelf and label this section, too.

Sort through your newspapers and magazines. Check the dates and come up with a rule of what is reasonable to let go of. For example, your rule might be, "I'll recycle anything that's older than two years because I haven't gotten around to reading it." If you would like to read a particular newspaper or magazine, mark it with the date six months from now in black permanent marker. If by that date you did not get to read it, it's time to let it go. Place all keepers in a basket near your recliner or sofa.

MOVIES AND GAMES

Sort through your collection of movies. Look through each DVD and VHS cassette whether wrapped or unwrapped. Determine which ones you want to keep, and donate the remaining ones. You can donate to local charities, senior centers, libraries, used bookstores, and other locations. Set up shelves to hold your movies or utilize the storage in your entertainment center. If your entertainment center does not have drawers, you can use decorative baskets to hold your favorite movies.

Next, look at all your games to see if there is a need to keep them all. Board games and puzzles that still have their pieces can be donated. Video games and video game consoles can be donated to various used bookstores and secondhand stores, or if they are in great condition, you can inquire about selling them. All keepers can be contained together on shelves, in drawers, or in labeled bins in the storage area of your home.

COZY ITEMS

Your living room may be the area of the home where you like to unwind, read a book, watch TV, or drink a cup of cocoa. Set up decorative baskets that slide under your coffee table to hold your blankets and throws when you are not using them. Or you can purchase a storage ottoman to hold these cozy items and to serve as a decorative addition to your living room.

PHOTOGRAPHS

Sorting through photos can be an incredibly difficult task because of their sentimental value. You may be holding on to certain photos to start scrapbooking. For now, gather the photos around the house to keep them contained in a protective bin. When you get the chance, you can organize them into photo albums or set up an electronic photo album. Coming back to scrapbooking can be a great way to practice self-care later.

TOYS

If children live in your home, create designated areas for toys that are being kept, like a toy chest or shelves with cubbies. It's a good idea to store some toys away and switch out the toys every so often to keep kids interested. Remind them to put their toys back in the designated area after play.

PET GOODIES

Let's not forget our fur babies! Gather a basket to keep all bones and toys contained to eliminate tripping hazards and so you can provide a toy to your pet with ease instead of searching the home or buying duplicates. Toys that are tearing and bones that are splintered can cause choking and other medical complications. Discard anything that can place your pets at risk.

HOBBY CORNER

Sewing, quilting, crocheting, or other types of creative endeavor may be an activity you enjoyed that your clutter interfered with. It's time to reclaim your hobby! Purchase organizing inserts and compartments to keep all your materials together according to their category. Set up your area and continue to perfect your craft.

COUCH AND CHAIRS

Keep your couch and chairs clear of objects that don't belong on them. A few throw pillows and a throw blanket are nice. Reroute any items that don't fall into that category. Work to maintain your seating areas so that you can enjoy them and guests you invite over will be comfortable.

COFFEE TABLE AND END TABLES

Coffee and end tables are decorative pieces of furniture that can add flair to any living room. They can also be used to organize your space. Some have open areas where you can place baskets to house movies, books, blankets/throws, and various electronics. A decorative tray can sit on the surface of the coffee table to hold remote controls, coasters, gaming controls, or a book. Add a nice bowl in the center of your tray to house smaller items, like a notepad and pens. If you have drawers in your end tables or coffee table, use the space to hold items you use regularly in your living room. Reroute all other items to their proper homes.

Bedroom

PATHWAYS

Maintain clear pathways throughout your bedroom. Gather up anything that's on the floor and sort through it. Once you've found homes for your "keep" items, start routinely putting them away and getting them off the floor as you come across them. Clearer pathways not only ensure safely but also help you feel more positive about the work you are doing.

BED

When was the last time you enjoyed a restful night of sleep in your bed? Getting a good night's rest promotes physical and mental health. Declutter your bed by sorting any items you've collected there, and once it's clear, put on fresh sheets. Try to get in the habit of keeping your bed clear to get that restful night's sleep you deserve. Set boundaries between you and your stuff. When bedtime approaches, reroute any items on your bed to their proper homes each night.

CLOTHING

I'm going to address your closet and dresser drawers separately, but first I want to discuss your clothing in general. After you've sorted your clothing and separated out anything that you don't see yourself wearing again, try on the rest and look at yourself in a full-length mirror. Ask yourself the following questions:

- Does it still fit?

- Is it still in style?

- Is it my style?

- Am I comfortable in it?

- Does it need any repairs, and is it worth repairing?

- When will I repair it?

- Do I have something similar? If so, which piece do I like more?

- How long has it been since I wore it? Why?

After you've answered these questions, reevaluate and donate any items you don't see yourself wearing again. Use this same process for your shoes.

Seasonal Sorting

Twice a year (spring and fall), sort through your closets, drawers, and shoes to quickly pick out items you feel comfortable donating. You'll be surprised how easily you can part with items the second time around. Statements like "I don't know why I kept this" might come up. Trust your intuition and allow yourself to let go. Generate a rule such as if you haven't worn a seasonal item within the last year, you can let go of it. Chances are, you will likely not wear it again.

DRESSER

Remove everything from your dresser drawers (or one drawer at a time to keep it more manageable) and sort your items into "keep," "donate," and "discard" piles. Have a container handy to hold anything that isn't clothing. Later, you can sort through those items. Put all your "keep" clothing back with categories in mind, such as pajamas in one drawer, workout clothes in another, and undergarments and socks in another. Fold the items and place them in their designated drawers.

Label the inside of your drawers, marking what category belongs inside that drawer. For some people with attention-span difficulties, it can be helpful to label the drawers according to the activities for which the clothing is used. For example, pajamas can be labeled *sleep* and workout clothing can be labeled *exercise*. Do what works best for you.

Also, as you organize your dresser drawers, pair up your socks to save yourself time. Discard socks without a partner and those that have seen better days. Continue the routine of pairing your socks after they have been laundered and put them back in their "home."

CLOSET

Remove everything from your closet, including anything that is on the floor, and sort your items into "keep," "donate," and "discard" categories. Hang all the "keep" clothing on hangers. Pay attention if you are trying to jam clothing in your closet. Overstuffing your closet will make it difficult for you to locate what you want to wear and will compromise your efforts to keep things hanging. If there's no room left, you might fall back in the habit of setting clothes down elsewhere in your bedroom or even around your home. If you notice this scenario happening, try to pare down your clothing a bit further. Here are additional tips:

- Get rid of excess hangers. If wire hangers are clean and in good condition, you can donate them to local dry cleaners or charities, but call ahead to confirm. If you need additional hangers, get strong slimline hangers, which take up less space than bulky hangers.

- Use hanging organizational dividers for bulky items. I am a fan of "cubbies" to hold things that take up a lot of space, like sweaters and hoodies. Some organizational dividers have side holders for belts, bags, and shoes.

- Hang hooks on the inside of your closet if you have wall space. These hooks can hold scarves, belts, and even hats to help you optimize your closet space even further. If you don't have wall space, you can place these items in bins.

- Organize clothing by category. Keeping similar items grouped together (for example, long-sleeved shirts, short-sleeved shirts, jackets, suits, dresses, etc.) will make it easier to locate items when you need them. You may want to organize your clothing by season, as well, placing the in-season clothing in an area of the closet that's more accessible.

- Use shoes racks or bins and boxes inside your closet to keep your shoes contained and organized. Get in the habit of putting your shoes back in their spot.

- Reroute any luggage/suitcases that you don't use frequently to your storage area to make more room for your clothing.

NIGHTSTAND

Limit what goes on top of your nightstand to items you need or use regularly at night—examples include reading glasses, a book you are reading, phone and phone charger, and alarm clock. Sort through any items that don't fit into that category. If your nightstand has drawers, determine how best to use them for storage and for things you regularly reach for in bed. Perhaps your nightstand drawer will hold a flashlight, a journal and pen, tissues, and so on. Label each drawer with the category of what you decide belongs in there.

BEDROOM SURFACES

For many, our bedrooms serve as our space of sanctuary and solitude. A cluttered bedroom can make us feel more stressed out and overwhelmed, which can impact your sleep cycle. Reclaim your bedroom as a place to rest and recover. Surfaces in your bedroom—the top of your dresser and your nightstand, shelves, entertainment center, chairs, and so on—should hold only items you value (decorative items) and everyday items you need to access, like a box of tissues or a jewelry box.

Bathroom

LINEN CLOSET

Although your linen closet may not technically be in your bathroom, I've placed it in this category since this is where we tend to keep towels and other bathroom-related items. I've notice that linen closets are underutilized storage areas; they can also be one of the least organized places in your home. Take the following steps to tackle your linen closet:

1. Open your linen closet and visually scan what's in there.

2. Jot down the categories of items that are currently in your linen closet (towels, washcloths, blankets, etc.).

3. Count how many of each category currently lives in your linen closet.

4. Closely estimate how many of each category you are currently using.

5. Remove the items from each shelf of the closet. Sort these items into "keep," "discard," and "donate" piles.

6. Come up with a rule of how many is a reasonable number per category—be realistic. How many sets of sheets, towels, and so forth do you really need? Challenge yourself to make decisions based on logic instead of allowing your emotions to be the boss.

7. Donate anything that is in good condition that you feel you can part with. Donate gently used towels and linens to local animal shelters and humane societies. Donate gently used blankets and linens to your local homeless shelter or women's center.

8. Label the shelves by their categories—for example, "Towels," "Sheets," and "Blankets." Place bulkier items, like pillows and comforters, on either the top or lowest shelf.

9. Fold and stack the items. Avoid creating leaning stacks or overly packing your closet to prevent items from toppling down.

TOWEL RACK

If you hang decorative towels on your towel rack that only guests are supposed to use, treat yourself as a guest and use them! I understand it can be a challenge because I grew up in a home where the decorative towels were reserved for guests. However, you deserve to enjoy your beautiful towels! Decorative towels that are not in use can be an additional category in your linen closet. The towel(s) you use daily can be kept on your shower towel rack if you have one.

TOILETRIES

Soap, shampoo, body lotion, hair tonic, perfume, body spray, moisturizer, shaving lotion, and so on—these items can really pile up. Products such as lotions and ointments whose expirations dates have passed should be discarded. If there's no expiration date and you are on the fence about a product, consider the following:

- Is the texture of the product a normal consistency? Do you notice any discoloration or hardening? Is it almost gone?

- Perfumes and body sprays lose their fragrance over time. Test to see if it is even a fragrance you are still attracted to. (Smell a handful of coffee beans or grounds between sniffing fragrances to keep your senses sharp, and take breaks to avoid headaches.)

- Discard old sunscreen (it's good for only one year after purchase).

MAKEUP

Do you have an abundance of makeup and other beauty products that you've used only half of, if that? Sort through your makeup and discard questionable items along with those you haven't used in years. Opened and used makeup can be a breeding ground for bacteria. Toss out mascara that has been opened and is over a year old to avoid bacterial eye infections. Some experts advise throwing out mascara three to six months after opening it. Use your judgment and maintain caution. If cosmetics are discolored, smell foul, or have a too-hard or too-soft consistency—it's time to let them go. With items that seem okay but you haven't used in a while, ask yourself if you are really going to use it again.

Once you've decided what to keep, gather clear organizers to store your makeup and products in, and be sure to label each accordingly. You can choose cosmetics organizers or even sectioned trays. Makeup bags hide what's inside, so you might forget what's in there and not use the product(s).

BATHROOM CABINET AND VANITY

Work on keeping your bathroom counters clear by fully utilizing your cabinets and vanity drawers. Place organizational bins in your cabinets and vanity drawers to keep categories separated and organized. Consider the following:

- Store bathroom cleaning products in their own bin under the sink or in a bin in your linen closet if you don't have an under-the-sink area.

- Use clear jars for cotton swabs, cotton balls, and makeup brushes.

- Use small organizational dividers to keep products such as foundation and lotions upright.

- Use organizational bins to divide categories (hairbrushes, blow-dryer, etc.).

- Install shelves above your toilet for additional storage of items, like a spare roll of toilet paper, a body fragrance, soap, and folded/stacked hand towels.

- Store shaving cream canisters, hair spray, and other aerosols away from baseboard heaters or other sources of extreme heat.

LAUNDRY BIN

In some homes, the laundry bin is in the bathroom. Others might keep one in their bedroom or elsewhere in the house. Wherever you keep yours, it helps to have two bins (some have a middle divider) to keep your clothing separated into colors and whites for easy upkeep. Do the laundry as soon as the bins fill up to keep them from overflowing. Follow the same rule even if you have only one laundry bin.

MEDICINE CABINET

Remove all contents from your medicine cabinet and sort through them. Collect all usable items and pile them together (for example, first-aid supplies). Discard all questionable items, like old antibiotic ointments, loose cotton swabs, gunky nail polish, and old toothbrushes (which should be replaced every three months). Place all "keep" items in narrow holders and put them back inside your medicine cabinet.

Check expiration dates of all prescriptions and over-the-counter medications. Discard anything that has expired. (Whether discarding or storing, make sure that children and pets cannot access them.) To dispose of prescription medication, contact your local public health department for safe disposal. The same rule applies for used syringes and sharps (devices with sharp points and edges). You can also sub-scribe to an affordable, prepaid medical waste company to pick up all medical sharps in a company-supplied sealed container.

SHOWER AND BATHTUB

Items that you use daily (shampoo, conditioner, soap, and bodywash, for instance) can be stored in the shower or bathtub if you have shelf space or a shower caddy. Otherwise, remove all the other supplies and items you use to get ready and put them in their identified homes. Leave the shower/tub empty and refrain from using these areas for storage. If you currently store excess items there, sort through them and find alternative homes for all retained items.

Before lining your wastebasket, place an extra bag or two at the bottom. This way, when you remove the trash, you'll have another bag handy.

Office

DAILY MAIL

Mail comes to our homes on a regular basis and requires constant maintenance. Place an empty container on a surface that your mail typically gets dumped on. It can be a small basket or even a shoebox without its lid. Use it to contain all incoming mail, and then set aside time to sort it into categories:

- **Junk mail:** Dispose of all "junk" mail immediately without opening it.

- **Action mail:** Use a labeled bin or hanging mail organizer for all mail that requires attention and that you must take action on, such as bills, tax forms, a jury duty summons, and invitations. Keep this type of mail separate from ordinary mail to help you avoid forgetting to pay a bill on time or to report for jury duty.

- **Catalogs, magazines, and newspapers:** Mark magazines and catalogs you plan to read at your leisure with a date six months from the day you received it. At the end of that six-month period, if you haven't read them, it is time to recycle them. Place them in an identified drawer or magazine basket. Each time the drawer or basket fills up, sort through it again. (Keep in mind that the news is also available online.) If you are consistently receiving magazines, catalogs, and newspapers that you are not reading and they continue to clutter up your space, take the time to unsubscribe.

- **Ordinary mail:** Address it as soon as you can.

PAPERWORK

Paperwork is a common complaint for people with clutter. File important documents away rather than letting them pile up. A filing cabinet or accordion folder is a good way to store necessary paperwork and personal documents. Label the file folders or accordion dividers by category. Sample categories include taxes, car insurance and title, medical insurance, and homeowner's insurance.

But what is "necessary" paperwork? Turn to outside sources to get a general idea of what you should keep and what you don't need to hold on to. For example, an outreach worker at your local senior center can address your inquiries about what you should keep regarding Medicare, health insurance, and Social Security. Your accountant or the person who helps file your taxes can provide guidance on what is necessary to save for tax purposes. Most professionals advise to file this paperwork for seven years.

Social workers and caseworkers at your primary care physician's office can also assist with questions regarding medical plan information and what is necessary to keep. When in doubt, ask yourself if the document is replaceable or if you can obtain a legitimate copy if you had to. If the answer is no, keep the document.

DESK

Keep your desk surface clear by making use of your desk drawers. Keep only the necessities visible, like your computer, printer, pens in a pen holder, and phone. Use a desk organizer for key materials you would like to keep reachable, such as paper, notepads, and a calculator. Use desk inserts to keep your other office supplies organized, as well. Place all similar items together (for example, paperclips, rubber bands, sticky notes, and staples). As you come across paperclips and rubber bands around the house, get in the habit of putting them in their designated home. Gather all your pens and pencils and sort through them. Determine if the pens still function and if the pencils are still in good condition. Place all working pens and pencils in a cup or container on top of your office desk, and dispose of the others.

Garage, Basement, Attic, and/or Storage Room

LAUNDRY AREA

In many homes, the washer and dryer are in the basement, but you may have a separate laundry room. Start by sorting your laundry supplies into "keep," "discard," and "donate" groups. If you don't already have an area in your laundry room to hold your supplies, install shelves to hold detergent, fabric softener, dryer sheets, and other laundry-related products. Avoid piling up soiled laundry on the floor next to your washer and dryer by using a laundry basket.

Use Pallets

If your storage area is subject to minor flooding or dampness, use plastic storage pallets, which you can likely find at your local hardware store. (Some grocery stores will let you have their used pallets for free.) You can place your storage bins on top of the pallets to further protect the items from moisture. Stack your bins side by side and on top of each other. Remember, don't stack too high.

DECORATIONS

Gather all holiday and seasonal decorations, sort them, and store what you are keeping in labeled, waterproof storage bins according to their occasion—for example, specific religious holidays, specific seasons, Independence Day, Halloween, and so on. After you've decorated for the season or holiday, notice which decorations you used and which you didn't use. If you haven't used them, it may be a clue to donate them.

UTILITY SHELVES

If you don't already have utility shelves, install them in your storage area for additional storage. If your storage area is accessible (as opposed to a hard-to-get-to attic), you can keep bulk cleaning supplies here, seasonal pots/pans/serving ware, and other bulky items. Be sure to label each shelf to identify what belongs there to prompt you to put it back.

HARDWARE AND CLEANING TOOLS

Sort through your tools (hammers, wrenches, screwdrivers, etc.), garden/lawn supplies (weed whacker, shovels, etc.), and cleaning supplies (brooms, mops, dusters, mop buckets, etc.). Install sturdy wall hooks with labels of what belongs there for any items you can hang to keep your floor space clear. Group like items together so you can easily locate an item you need when you need it.

SEASONAL SHOES AND GARDEN WEAR

Sort through your seasonal shoes (snow or rain boots, gardening clogs, etc.) and any garden wear (gloves, sun visor, etc.). Store the shoes in a wall rack, door rack, or shoe rack, and place all garden wear in a labeled container.

BULK PET FOOD AND PET NEEDS

Store any bulk pet food in a large, sealed container. Label the container with the expiration date of the food you are placing inside. Place this container on a pallet or utility shelf to protect it from moisture. Sort through leashes, collars, and harnesses and hang them on hooks. Place other items you've decided to keep, such as a collapsible water bowl and jackets, in a container on your utility shelf. Dispose of or donate unwanted pet supplies.

SUITCASES

As mentioned in the bedroom section (see page 126), store away luggage that you don't use frequently rather than leave it in your closets.

Gather all suitcases throughout your home, sort them, and place the keepers in your storage area. Place smaller pieces of luggage inside the larger ones to save space. Put the suitcases on a pallet for safekeeping. Removing these bulky items from the main part of your home makes more room in your closets for items you use more frequently.

PAINTS AND HAZARDOUS WASTE

Sort through all your paint cans and potentially hazardous waste, like paint thinners and other chemical-laden products. (Check what's considered hazardous waste with your local waste management and/or public health department.) Determine if the items are still good. Rusty canisters likely indicate that the items are old and should be disposed of. If you are keeping paints, label the tops of the cans with the paint color and which room they were used in or the purpose they serve. Leftover paints, paint thinners, and old paints can be disposed of by dropping them off at your local hardware store for free disposal (call ahead). You can also purchase small packets of paint hardeners that make these products safe for general waste disposal. Contact your local waste management or public health department for hazardous waste removal or designated days for drop-off.

"Junk" Drawer

MISCELLANEOUS ITEMS

Pull out everything from your junk drawer. Sort the items and discard anything that's garbage. Anything that has a home elsewhere should be rerouted to that area. For example, keep paper clips in your desk drawer; there's no reason to have duplicate homes for items. Figure out what you want to keep in this drawer and why. Then, place drawer inserts appropriate for your drawer so that you can quickly organize your miscellaneous items. Remember to keep similar items together.

BATTERIES

Keep good and usable batteries contained. Discard questionable batteries that are dented and/or soiled. You can dispose of batteries at your local public health department.

BULBS AND SMALL ELECTRONICS

Keep bulbs protected and contained, preferably in their packaging and together. If you have spare bulbs and electronics that are not functioning, contact your local waste management for disposal. There is no need to keep extra cords and electronic items if you aren't sure what they are for. There are some collection services for old electronics. Do a little research to find one in your area.

TRASH

There is no need to organize the actual trash in your drawer. If you think an item is trash (an expired coupon, gum wrappers, or old or duplicate menus, for instance), discard it. Other garbage might include unidentifiable keys, combination locks without the combination, broken sunglasses, a battered keychain, or a lighter with no fluid.

Tips for a Small Space

For smaller apartments, every square foot counts. To make your apartment functional, some creativity is required. Here are a few ideas:

- If you don't have a closet or have limited closet space for clothing, use a slim clothing rack.
- Add wall hooks in your entryway to hold coats, scarves, umbrellas, keys, and so forth, especially if you don't have a main hallway closet or if you use it to store other prime items.
- Add sturdy floating shelves to any wall space in your living areas to hold decorations, books, and movies.
- Sturdy floating shelves can also be a great way of maximizing your kitchen space. You can use them to hold plates, cups, or dried goods. If you are worried about aesthetics, place the dried goods in decorative clear jars, appropriately labeled.
- Place organizing baskets on the tops of your kitchen cabinets and refrigerator to house excess items. Make sure you use baskets that can be washed in case something spills.
- Place your trash barrel under your kitchen sink to maximize your floor space.

Conclusion

Congratulations! You are well on your way to achieving an organized home. With patience and continued effort, you will see more progress and maintain your gains. Remember, there are factors that led to how your home got to its cluttered state. It will not all get done in one evening. Learning to live a life free from clutter is a process, so be patient with yourself. You can do this!

Self-Care Tip

Now that you have a clear countertop, cook a nice meal for yourself. Revisit a recipe or try a new one and treat yourself. Better yet, invite someone over to enjoy that meal with you. Bon appétit!

CHAPTER EIGHT

How to Make New Habits Stick

Congratulations on getting this far in your journey! The lifestyle changes you're aiming for are worthwhile and rewarding, but chances are you'll occasionally experience setbacks. This chapter provides strategies for staying the course and developing lasting ways to make your new clutter-free habits stick. What happens if you fall off track? This chapter tells you how to pick up where you left off, and most important, it reminds you to be compassionate toward yourself. Achieving an organized lifestyle is a journey that requires physical and emotional maintenance.

10 Tips for Staying the Course

Here are some tips you can implement that incorporate the strategies you've learned throughout this book. These tips will help you stay on track with sustaining organization, remaining in control, and achieving the clutter-free, organized lifestyle you desire.

1. CHECK IN WITH YOURSELF REGULARLY

Like any unfamiliar journey, setbacks are not unusual. Remember that keeping yourself clutter-free and organized is a new experience for you. You are trying to make a change after a long period of things remaining the same in your life. You are trying to overcome physical clutter, mental distress, and self-doubt. Just because you organize doesn't mean that things will automatically fall into place. Your journey will require continued effort, such as keeping up with putting items back in the areas you designated for them as well as combating unhelpful thoughts when they arise.

If you are starting to feel overwhelmed and notice yourself backsliding, take the time to sit with your thoughts and evaluate the vulnerabilities that are contributing to the regression. Ask yourself the following:

- Are you noticing a worsening of your mood? Are you becoming more depressed or anxious? Reach out to your therapist/psychiatrist or investigate connecting with one.

- Are you feeling pressure from family or friends? Take the time to sit with them in a neutral setting and discuss boundaries. Say that you are working on this journey and the additional pressure is keeping you at a standstill. See if they would be willing to help you if you can move forward in a collaborative way.

Whatever the case may be, external factors outside of the clutter may be connected to your falling off course. Explore what these factors may be and talk it out so that you can once again move forward.

2. SCHEDULE SESSIONS WITH YOURSELF

Keep up with routine sorting and maintaining your uncluttered spaces by making appointments with yourself on your calendar—even if you think you have a pretty good handle on the situation. Allocate time to sort, organize, and maintain to help you continue to practice keeping your home in a manageable state. Putting off sorting or returning items to their homes can lead to items reaccumulating to the point where you might begin to avoid taking care of them. Spend the extra few minutes every day to put things away, wash the dishes, hang up your clothes, open your mail, and work on your projects. Remind yourself that you did something good today that helped you continue to achieve your goals.

3. LOCATE OUTSIDE SUPPORT

If you haven't already, start exploring outside support systems. Join a support group and connect with a mental health professional and/or professional organizer. Connecting with social supports helps decrease the feeling of isolation associated with this issue. You can learn to evaluate and overcome setbacks together. Mental health professionals can help you explore the mental roadblocks that are preventing you from maintaining your gains—and you both can find ways to remove the barriers to change. Professional organizers will help you stay on track with ideas and reminders to sustain an organized lifestyle.

4. BE OPEN TO REEVALUATING YOUR GOALS

Take the time to reflect through this book, particularly chapters 3 and 4, which highlight goals and motivation. As time goes on, your goals will likely change. Therefore, you might need to reevaluate and develop new goals that make sense for where you are now. New goals can motivate you to continue the work you've been doing. Perhaps you've set a goal to eliminate excess paper from your home, and now that you've achieved that goal, you might want to figure out a better way to organize the papers you do keep. Or perhaps you set a goal to get your kitchen to the point where you can move around freely, find the utensils you need, and prepare your meals. Your next goal might be to have a friend over for a meal you will create.

5. REVISIT ROOMS YOU'VE ALREADY ORGANIZED

After you have sorted and organized various areas in your home, revisit these areas to see if there is more that you can do. Oftentimes, the second time you sort in a target room, the easier it is to let some things go. At minimum, sort designated areas once or twice a year. Pick an area and work on just that section to see if there are other items you would like to part with. Your opinion of certain items may shift over time. When you've sifted through your belongings, stick with the organizational strategies described in chapter 7 to keep things contained and accessible.

6. KEEP YOUR TIMER HANDY

It's so easy to lose track of time and get lost in a task or distracted from it. The strategy of timing yourself is one that will come in handy as you move forward. For instance, if you set a timer to sort through your mail, it can keep you from getting lost in reading a catalog. You can read the catalog after the timer has gone off. Any time you set out to sort, organize, or maintain your space, your timer can help keep you on task.

7. KEEP SURFACES CLEAR

Keep all the surfaces throughout your home clear of clutter by routinely putting items where they belong. If you are bringing in new purchases, put the items away instead of leaving them somewhere "for now." Keep a rag and cleaner available to wipe surfaces down regularly. A pleasant aroma and the glistening sheen of a cleaned surface can motivate you to not let things pile up again. Remind yourself of the importance of cleared surfaces, such as for meal preparation on your counters, the ability to sit down at your table and enjoy your coffee or a nice meal, the ability to find something when needed, and having a space that represents your aesthetic style.

8. ASK DECISION-MAKING QUESTIONS

Always ask yourself the decision-making questions you learned in chapter 3 when it comes to keeping or acquiring something. Explore your personal reasons for keeping an item by carefully reviewing and answering each question. The same idea applies to any anticipated purchases that would be coming into your home. Once you've made a decision, take steps to see it through. If your decision feels like it's causing you any guilt, it might be time to reevaluate the decision to determine if it's right for you.

9. KEEP IT SIMPLE

Keep your efforts simple. There is no need to reinvent the wheel. Stick to simplified and limited sorting categories that make sense for the activity at hand. Remember the rule: Keep, discard, or donate. Each sorting session, organizational exercise, or daily upkeep should not be a marathon. Set your timer, keep your personal commitment to yourself, and do not create more work than necessary.

10. CELEBRATE YOU, ALWAYS

It is not selfish to take a moment to congratulate yourself on your achievements, no matter how small. Take the time to reflect on your efforts. Look at your before-and-after photos. Your home may look like a very different space than when you first started this journey. Be kind to yourself and reward yourself. By rewarding yourself, you are engaging in routine self-care. Use the self-care tips throughout the book as a reminder. Continue to engage in alternative pleasurable activities to rejuvenate yourself.

Conclusion

Congratulations! You are well on your way toward using these skills and strategies to implement lifelong change. Refer back to this chapter whenever you are feeling stuck. Your journey of achieving both a mentally and physically organized lifestyle will require patience, perseverance, and continued maintenance. You might experience periods of great success and moments of diminished motivation. Review your goals, reflect on your strategies, and make a commitment to yourself. You deserve a life of uncluttered happiness.

Resources

Mental Health Provider Directories

Anxiety and Depression Association of America: adaa.org

Association for Behavioral and Cognitive Therapies: abct.org

International OCD Foundation: iocdf.org

Psychology Today: psychologytoday.com/us

Support Group Information

Buried in Treasures workshops: mutual-support.com/the_buried_in _treasures_workshop

Buried in Treasures: Help for Compulsive Acquiring, Saving, and Hoarding, by David Tolin, Randy Frost, and Gail Steketee

Clutterers Anonymous: clutterersanonymous.org

Professional Organizers

National Association of Productivity & Organizing Professionals (NAPO): napo.net

Online Support and Other Websites

The Clutter Movement: thecluttermovement.com

The Clutter Movement Individual Support Facebook group: facebook.com/groups/TheClutterMovementIndividualSupport

Hoarding Task Force Network: facebook.com/groups/HoardingTask
ForceNetwork

Institute for Challenging Disorganization: challengingdisorganization.org

Mutual Support Consulting: mutual-support.com/what_we_offer

Animal Hoarding Information

Cummings School of Veterinary Medicine at Tufts University:
vet.tufts.edu/hoarding

For Children of Hoarders

Children of Hoarders: childrenofhoarders.com

Coming Clean: A Memoir, by Kimberly Rae Miller

For Family Members

The Clutter Movement: thecluttermovement.com

Clutter Movement Family Support: facebook.com/groups
/TheClutterMovementFamilySupport/

*Digging Out: Helping Your Loved One Manage Clutter, Hoarding, and
Compulsive Acquiring*, by Michael Tompkins and Tamara L. Hartl

References

Abramowitz, J. S., J. D. Huppert, A. B. Cohen, D. F. Tolin, and S. P. Cahill. "Religious Obsessions and Compulsions in a Nonclinical Sample: The Penn Inventory of Scrupulosity (PIOS)." *Behaviour Research and Therapy* 40, no. 7 (July 2002): 824–38. doi.org/10.1016/S0005-7967(01)00070-5.

American Psychiatric Association. *Diagnostic and Statistical Manual of Mental Disorders,* 5th ed. Washington, DC: American Psychiatric Association, 2013.

Aslett, Don. *Clutter's Last Stand: It's Time to De-junk Your Life!* Cincinnati, OH: Writer's Digest Books, 1984.

Baird, Lori, ed. *Cut the Clutter and Stow the Stuff: The Q.U.I.C.K. Way to Bring Lasting Order to Household Chaos.* Dublin, NH: Yankee Publishing, 2002.

Berry, Colin, Gary Patronek, and Randall Lockwood. "Long-Term Outcomes in Animal Hoarding Cases." *Animal Law* 11, no. 1 (2005): 167–94. law.lclark.edu/law_reviews/animal_law_review/past_issues/volume_11.php.

Boddy, Jennifer, Patrick O'Leary, Ming-Sum Tsui, Chiu-Man Pak, and Duu-Chiang Wang. "Inspiring Hope through Social Work Practice." *International Social Work* 61, no. 4 (May 2017): 587–99. doi.org/10.1177/0020872817706408.

Boyle, Sally, Jitka Vseteckova, and Martyn Higgins. "Impact of Motivational Interviewing by Social Workers on Service Users: A Systematic Review." *Research on Social Work Practice* 29, no. 8 (February 2019): 863–75. doi.org/10.1177/1049731519827377.

Bratiotis, Christiana, Jennie Davidow, Katharine Glossner, and Gail Steketee. "Requests for Help with Hoarding: Who Needs What from Whom?" *Practice Innovations* 1, no. 1 (March 2016): 82–88. doi.org/10.1037/pri0000017.

Chang, Yu-Ping, Peggy Compton, Pamela Almeter, and Chester H. Fox. "The Effect of Motivational Interviewing on Prescription Opioid Adherence among Older Adults with Chronic Pain." *Perspectives in Psychiatric Care* 51, no. 3 (August 2014): 211–19. doi.org/10.1111/ppc.12082.

Chemolli, Emanuela, and Marylène Gagné. "Evidence against the Continuum Structure Underlying Motivation Measures Derived from Self-Determination Theory." *Psychological Assessment* 26, no. 2 (June 2014): 575–85. doi.org/10.1037/a0036212.

Cooke, Jo. *Understanding Hoarding*. London: Sheldon Press, 2017.

Crackau, Brit, Ira Loehrmann, Anne Zahradnik, Christiane Otto, Ulrich John, Gallus Bischof, and Hans-Jürgen Rumpf. "Measuring Readiness to Change for Problematic Consumption of Prescription Drugs: Development of an Adapted and Shortened Readiness to Change Questionnaire." *Addiction Research & Theory* 18, no. 1 (January 2010): 110–18. doi.org/10.3109/16066350802699310.

Cummings School of Veterinary Medicine at Tufts University. "Hoarding of Animals Research Consortium." Accessed March 10, 2020. vet.tufts.edu/hoarding/.

De Jong, Peter, and Insoo Kim Berg. *Interviewing for Solutions*. Belmont, CA: Nelson Education, 2012.

de Vries, Rivka M., and Richard D. Morey. "Bayesian Hypothesis Testing for Single-Subject Designs." *Psychological Methods* 18, no. 2 (June 2013): 165–85. doi.org/10.1037/a0031037.

Denning, Patt. *Practicing Harm Reduction Psychotherapy: An Alternative Approach to Addictions*. New York: Guilford Press, 2000.

Eckhardt, Christopher I., and Angela C. Utschig. "Assessing Readiness to Change among Perpetrators of Intimate Partner Violence: Analysis of Two Self-Report Measures." *Journal of Family Violence* 22, no. 5 (May 2007): 319–30. doi.org/10.1007/s10896-007-9088-9.

Frost, Randy O., and Gail Steketee. *Stuff: Compulsive Hoarding and the Meaning of Things.* New York: Houghton Mifflin Harcourt, 2010.

Frost, Randy O., Gary Patronek, and Elizabeth Rosenfield. "Comparison of Object and Animal Hoarding." *Depression and Anxiety* 3, no. 28 (October 2011): 885–91. doi: 10.1002/da.20826.

Frost, Randy O., and Rachel C. Gross. "The Hoarding of Possessions." *Behaviour Research and Therapy* 31, no. 4 (May 1993): 367–81. doi.org/10.1016/0005-7967(93)90094-B.

Grote, Nancy K., Allan Zuckoff, Holly Swartz, Sarah E. Bledsoe, and Sharon Geibel. "Engaging Women Who Are Depressed and Economically Disadvantaged in Mental Health Treatment." *Social Work* 52, no. 4 (October 2007): 295–308. doi.org/10.1093/sw/52.4.295.

Hampson, Margaret E., Richard E. Hicks, and Bruce D. Watt. "Exploring the Effectiveness of Motivational Interviewing in Re-engaging People Diagnosed with Severe Psychiatric Conditions in Work, Study, or Community Participation." *American Journal of Psychiatric Rehabilitation* 18, no. 3 (August 2015): 265–79. doi.org/10.1080/15487768 .2014.954158.

Kyrios, Michael, Christopher Mogan, Richard Moulding, Randy O. Frost, and Keong Yap, and Daniel B. Fassnacht. "The Cognitive–Behavioural Model of Hoarding Disorder: Evidence from Clinical and Non-clinical Cohorts." *Clinical Psychology & Psychotherapy* 25, no. 2 (March 2018): 311–21. doi: 10.1002/cpp.2164.

Lee, Christina S., Suzanne M. Colby, Damaris J. Rohsenow, Rosemarie Martin, Robert Rosales, Tonya Tavares McCallum, Luis Falcon, Joanna Almeida, and Dharma E. Cortés. "A Randomized Controlled Trial of Motivational Interviewing Tailored for Heavy Drinking Latinxs."

Journal of Consulting and Clinical Psychology 87, no. 9 (September 2019): 815–30. doi.org/10.1037/ccp0000428.

Lewis, Todd F., Mary F. Larson, and James S. Korcuska. "Strengthening the Planning Process of Motivational Interviewing Using Goal Attainment Scaling." *Journal of Mental Health Counseling* 39, no. 3 (July 2017): 195–210. doi.org/10.17744/mehc.39.3.02.

Logan, Diane E., and G. Allen Marlatt. "Harm Reduction Therapy: A Practice-Friendly Review of Research." *Journal of Clinical Psychology* 66, no. 2 (February 2010): 201–14. doi.org/10.1002/jclp.20669.

Luke, Carter, Gary Patronek, Arnold Arluke, Jane Nathanson, Edward Messner, Gail Steketee, Randy Frost and Michelle Papazian. "Press Reports of Animal Hoarding." *Society and Animals* 10, no. 2 (January 2002): 113–35. doi.org/10.1163/156853002320292282.

Marlatt, G. Alan, Mary E. Latimer, and Katie Witkiewitz, eds. *Harm Reduction: Pragmatic Strategies for Managing High-Risk Behaviors.* New York: Guilford Press, 2012.

Miller, Chris H., and Dawson W. Hedges. "Scrupulosity Disorder: An Overview and Introductory Analysis." *Journal of Anxiety Disorders* 22, no. 6 (August 2008): 1042–58. doi.org/10.1016/j.janxdis.2007.11.004.

Miller, William R., and Stephen Rollnick. *Motivational Interviewing: Helping People Change*, 3rd ed. New York: Guilford Press, 2012.

Morton, Gregg Riley. "Animal Hoarding in Florida: Addressing the Ongoing Animal, Human, and Public Health Crisis." *Florida Bar Journal* 91, no. 4 (April 2017): 30. floridabar.org/the-florida-bar-journal/animal-hoarding-in-florida-addressing-the-ongoing-animal-human-and-public-health-crisis/.

Muroff, Jordana, Patty Underwood, and Gail Steketee. *Group Treatment for Hoarding Disorder: Therapist Guide.* New York: Oxford University Press, 2014.

Olatunji, Bunmi O., Jonathan Stuart Abramowitz, Nathan L. Williams, Kevin M. Connolly, and Jeffrey M. Lohr. "Scrupulosity and Obsessive-Compulsive Symptoms: Confirmatory Factor Analysis and Validity of the Penn Inventory of Scrupulosity." *Journal of Anxiety Disorders* 21, no. 6 (2007): 771–87. doi.org/10.1016/j.janxdis.2006.12.002.

Paloski, Luis Henrique, Elisa Arrienti Ferreira, Dalton Breno Costa, María Laura del Huerto, Camila Rosa de Oliveira, Irani Iracema de Lima Argimon, and Tatiana Quarti Irigaray. "Animal Hoarding Disorder: A Systematic Review." *Psico* 48, no. 3 (September 2017): 243–49. doi.org/10.15448/1980-8623.2017.3.25325.

Patronek, Gary J. "Hoarding of Animals: An Under-Recognized Public Health Problem in a Difficult-to-Study Population." *Public Health Reports* 114, no. 1 (January–February 1999): 81–87. doi.org/10.1093/phr/114.1.81.

Patronek, Gary J., and Jane N. Nathanson. "A Theoretical Perspective to Inform Assessment and Treatment Strategies for Animal Hoarders." *Clinical Psychology Review* 29, no. 3 (April 2009): 274–81. doi.org/10.1016/j.cpr.2009.01.006.

Patronek, Gary J., Lynn Loar, and Jane N. Nathanson, eds. *Animal Hoarding: Strategies for Interdisciplinary Interventions to Help People, Animals, and Communities at Risk.* Boston: Hoarding of Animals Research Consortium, 2006.

Perreault, Michel, Marie-Christine Héroux, Noé Djawn White, Pierre Lauzon, Céline Mercier, and Michel Rousseau. "Treatment Retention and Evolution of Clientele in a Low-Threshold Methadone Program in Montreal." *Canadian Journal of Public Health* 98, no. 1 (January 2007): 33–36. researchgate.net/publication/6525466_Treatment_retention_and_evolution_of_clients_of_a_low-threshold_methadone_program_in_Montreal.

Raines, Amanda M., Jesus Chavarria, Nicholas P. Allan, Nicole A. Short, and Norman B. Schmidt. "Hoarding Behaviors and Alcohol Use: The Mediating Role of Emotion Dysregulation." *Substance Use & Misuse* 52, no. 13 (June 2017): 1684–91. doi.org/10.1080/10826084.2017.1305414.

Rose, Sheldon D., and Hee-Suk Chang. "Motivating Clients in Treatment Groups." *Social Work with Groups* 33, nos. 2–3 (February 2007): 260–77. doi.org/10.1080/01609510903551241.

Rosmarin, David H., Steven Pirutinsky, and Jedidiah Siev. "Recognition of Scrupulosity and Non-religious OCD by Orthodox and Non-Orthodox Jews." *Journal of Social and Clinical Psychology* 29, no. 8 (2010): 930–44. doi.org/10.1521/jscp.2010.29.8.930.

Shaeffer, Megan. "The Social Context of Hoarding Behavior: Building a Foundation for Sociological Study." *Sociology Compass* 11, no. 4 (April 2017): e12472. doi.org/10.1111/soc4.12472.

Simmel, Georg. "Fashion." *The American Journal of Sociology* vol. LXII (6): 541–58. http://sites.middlebury.edu/individualandthesociety /files/2010/09/Simmel.fashion.pdf.

Sowards, Kathryn A., Kathleen O'Boyle, and Marsha Weissman. "Inspiring Hope, Envisioning Alternatives: The Importance of Peer Role Models in a Mandated Treatment Program for Women." *Journal of Social Work Practice in the Addictions* 6, no. 4 (2006): 55–70. doi.org/10.1300/J160v06n04_04.

Steketee, Gail, ed. *The Oxford Handbook of Obsessive Compulsive and Spectrum Disorders.* New York: Oxford University Press, 2012.

Steketee, Gail, and Randy O. Frost. *Compulsive Hoarding and Acquiring: Therapist Guide.* New York: Oxford University Press, 2007.

Steketee, Gail, and Randy O. Frost. *Compulsive Hoarding and Acquiring: Workbook.* New York: Oxford University Press, 2007.

Steketee, Gail, and Randy O. Frost. *Treatment for Hoarding Disorder: Therapist Guide.* New York: Oxford University Press, 2013.

Thomas, Geralin, ed. *From Hoarding to Hope: Understanding People Who Hoard and How to Help Them.* Cary, NC: MetroZing Publishing, 2015.

Tolin, David, Randy O. Frost, and Gail Steketee. *Buried in Treasures: Help for Compulsive Acquiring, Saving, and Hoarding.* New York: Oxford University Press, 2014.

Tolin, David F., Bethany M. Wootton, Hannah C. Levy, Lauren S. Hallion, Blaise L. Worden, Gretchen J. Diefenbach, James Jaccard, and Michael C. Stevens. "Efficacy and Mediators of a Group Cognitive–Behavioral Therapy for Hoarding Disorder: A Randomized Trial." *Journal of Consulting and Clinical Psychology* 87, no. 7 (July 2019): 590–602. doi.org/10.1037/ccp0000405.

Tolin, David F., Blaise L. Worden, Bethany M. Wootton, and Christina M. Gilliam. *CBT for Hoarding Disorder: A Group Therapy Program Therapist's Guide.* Hoboken, NJ: John Wiley & Sons, 2017.

Tompkins, Michael A. *Clinician's Guide to Severe Hoarding.* Oakland, CA: Springer Science+Business Media, 2015.

Tompkins, Michael A. "Working with Families of People Who Hoard: A Harm Reduction Approach." *Journal of Clinical Psychology* 67, no. 5 (May 2011): 497–506. doi.org/10.1002/jclp.20797.

Tompkins, Michael A., and Tamara L. Hartl. *Digging Out: Helping Your Loved One Manage Clutter, Hoarding, and Compulsive Acquiring.* Oakland, CA: New Harbinger Publications, 2009.

Torres, Ayse, Michael Frain, and Timothy N. Tansey. "The Impact of Motivational Interviewing Training on Rehabilitation Counselors: Assessing Working Alliance and Client Engagement. A Randomized Controlled Trial." *Rehabilitation Psychology* 64, no. 3 (August 2019): 328–38. doi.org/10.1037/rep0000267.

Ung, Jennifer E., Mary E. Dozier, Christiana Bratiotis, and Catherine R. Ayers. "An Exploratory Investigation of Animal Hoarding Symptoms in a Sample of Adults Diagnosed with Hoarding Disorder." *Journal of Clinical Psychology* 73, no. 9 (December 2016): 1114–25. doi.org/10.1002/jclp.22417.

van der Kaap-Deeder, Jolene, Maarten Vansteenkiste, Bart Soenens, Joke Verstuyf, Liesbet Boone, and Jos Smets. "Fostering Self-Endorsed Motivation to Change in Patients with an Eating Disorder: The Role of Perceived Autonomy Support and Psychological Need Satisfaction." *International Journal of Eating Disorders* 47, no. 6 (March 2014): 585–600. doi.org/10.1002/eat.22266.

Vansteenkiste, Maarten, and Kennon M. Sheldon. "There's Nothing More Practical Than a Good Theory: Integrating Motivational Interviewing and Self-Determination Theory." *British Journal of Clinical Psychology* 45, no. 1 (April 2006): 63–82.

Wallman, James. *Stuffocation: Why We've Had Enough of Stuff and Need Experience More Than Ever.* New York: Spiegel & Grau, 2015.

Walsh, Peter. *Enough Already! Clearing Mental Clutter to Become the Best You.* New York: Free Press, 2009.

Walsh, Peter. *How to Organize (Just About) Everything: More Than 500 Step-by-Step Instructions for Everything from Organizing Your Closets to Planning a Wedding to Creating a Flawless Filing System.* New York: Free Press, 2004.

Ware, Ciji. *Rightsizing Your Life: Simplifying Your Surroundings While Keeping What Matters Most.* New York: Springboard Press, 2007.

Wincze, Jeffrey P., Gail Steketee, and Randy O. Frost. "Categorization in Compulsive Hoarding." *Behaviour Research and Therapy* 45, no. 1 (January 2007): 63–72. doi.org/10.1016/j.brat.2006.01.012.

Index

Acknowledgments

SHORTLY AFTER MY UNDERGRADUATE STUDIES, I worked as a case manager conducting home visits with mainly older adults. I often encountered cluttered living environments that were affecting my clients' in-home service delivery. These services are intended to support the clients' continued ability to live independently in the community. What I recognized was not just the impact of services but, more important, their countless verbal expressions of shame related to their environment. Their statements highlighted their overall diminished hope that they would ever be able to kick their hoarding-related habits. I recognized that my knowledge of hoarding at the time was limited. I struggled to accept suggestions that my clients should just throw out their stuff. Although my knowledge of hoarding as a mental health issue was not expansive, I knew this approach was inappropriate and would have detrimental effects on my clients' overall well-being.

These experiences encouraged me to return to school to study mental health generally, and hoarding disorder specifically. While in graduate school, I completed my first-year field practicum at the North Shore Center for Hoarding and Clutter, where I still practice. During my initial internship, my mentor invited me into a world of seeing hoarding far beyond just the stuff. I therefore thank my mentor and predecessor, Marnie Matthews, for supporting my curiosities and desire to be a better clinical social worker. Thank you, Marnie, for entrusting me with directing the center that you dedicated a large portion of your life to create. I also thank Karen Sullivan, who makes up our two-person team at the center. She shows the same dedication to working with clients as we travel to various parts of Massachusetts to treat and advocate for clients looking to improve their lives. I thank my clients with whom I have worked and who have shown me their never-ending resilience, strength, and potential for living, despite adversities.

I thank my mother, a former social worker, a single mother, who raised me to always think of social justice values and ideals in supporting the people I work with. She raised me to think of people far beyond their psychological makeup to really consider how society shapes and influences our decisions. This book is a testament to my conviction that clinical social work is relevant in working with people who hoard and clutter by using psychologically informed, socially relevant concepts and environmental aspects to fully help and understand all people affected by clutter. I also want to thank my father, who continuously challenges me to remember that peer supports are one of the most undervalued aspects, critical to supporting lifelong recovery when working with folks in mental health and addictions. I thank my family for hugging me when I am down and for cheering me on—I would not be who I am without them.

My greatest thanks goes to my husband, Tim Dacey, who serves as a bright and passionate sociologist. His quirky, humorous, generous, thoughtful presence has enabled me to always reach for my potential while giving me space to write, study, travel, and live an independent life.

I want to thank my colleagues at the Simmons School of Social Work. I can proudly say that my development as a clinical social worker is a testament of my valuable experience and education at the nation's first school of social work. I thank my current professors and humble network of practitioners, policy makers, and academics in my current doctoral studies at Simmons University. I thank all of the influential researchers in the field, specifically, Dr. Randy Frost, Dr. Gail Steketee, and Dr. Michael Tompkins. Their expansive work has paved the way for my overall understanding and knowledge on the subject of hoarding and acquisition.

Finally, I thank the entire Callisto Media team for making the development of this book a reality. Specifically, I am thankful for the great editorial skills of Emily Angell and Carol Rosenberg, who read many, many drafts of this book.

About the Author

© Jayne Girodat

EILEEN DACEY, MSW, LCSW, is program director for the North Shore Center for Hoarding and Cluttering. She provides clinical in-home psychotherapy in treatment of hoarding disorder throughout eastern Massachusetts. In addition, Eileen facilitates support groups for individuals and family members affected by hoarding. She provides crisis management for individuals facing outside pressure, such as evictions and condemnations, related to hoarding behavior. She also serves as one of the few clinicians in Massachusetts who provide crisis management and psychotherapy for individuals demonstrating animal hoarding behavior.

Eileen provides presentations and trainings throughout the country on all aspects of hoarding and cluttering. She chairs the North Shore Hoarding Task Force and is a member of the Everett Hoarding Task Force, Cape Ann Hoarding Task Force, Boston Hoarding Task Force, and Statewide Steering Committee for Hoarding. She was influential in working with legislators to establish the legislative proclamation declaring Hoarding Disorder Awareness Week in the Commonwealth of Massachusetts. Eileen is also an advocate on the PAWS II (a bill to fight animal cruelty) commission in Massachusetts. She is a current doctoral student at Simmons School of Social Work with research interests surrounding the prevention and identification of animal hoarding as well as the development of clinical treatment and intervention for people who hoard animals.

Outside of her full-time work and schooling obligations, Eileen works part-time at an emergency room as a psychiatric triage clinician and volunteers with the American Red Cross as a disaster mental health clinician. When she is not working, she enjoys playing tennis both socially and competitively and spending time with her beagle, Darwin.